GRILLING
BEST-EVER GRILLS & BBQ RECIPES

GRILLING
BEST-EVER GRILLS & BBQ RECIPES

bay books

MEAL PLANNER

Use the following table to plan your best-ever Grills and Barbecue meal. The recipes have been grouped into appropriate classifications and the portion size of each recipe is clearly shown. Plan your meal and then turn to the appropriate page to find your clear and concise recipe together with a large-format picture of the finished dish.

SALADS, SNACKS & STARTERS

RECIPE	PAGE	PORTIONS
Garlic dip with crudites	12	4
Tzatziki	16	12
Tapenade	19	10
Baba ghannouj	23	10
Chicken salad with rocket and cannellini beans	27	4
Warm marinated mushroom salad	31	4
Tomato and bocconcini salad	35	4
Curly endive salad with crisp prosciutto and garlic croutons	39	6

BEEF, LAMB & PORK

RECIPE	PAGE	PORTIONS
Lamb souvlaki	63	4
Beef satay	47	4
Cheeseburgers with capsicum salsa	51	6
Beef fajitas	55	4–6
Beef kebabs with mint yoghurt dressing	56	8 skewers
Pepper steaks with horseradish sauce	107	4
Chilli beef burgers	68	4
Lamb with salsa verde and polenta wedges	108	4
Greek pepper lamb salad	112	4
Ginger-orange pork	137	6
Chilli lamb cutlets	141	4
Hoisin lamb with charred spring onion	152	4
Lamb kebabs	48	4
Chilli pork ribs	164	4–6

RECIPE	PAGE	PORTIONS
White bean salad with tuna	40	4–6
Barbecue vegetable and tofu kebabs	44	4
Vegetarian burgers with coriander garlic cream	60	10 burgers
Tuna skewers with Moroccan spices and chermoula	64	4
Tofu kebabs with miso pesto	67	4
Lamb pitta	71	4
Vegetarian skewers with basil couscous	75	4
Lamb souvlaki roll	88	4
Herb burgers	96	8 burgers
Spicy burgers with avocado salsa	100	6

RECIPE	PAGE	PORTIONS
Sesame and ginger beef	175	4
Beef with blue cheese butter	168	4
Pork with apple and onion wedges	188	4
Lamb chops with citrus pockets	171	4
Lamb cutlets with mint gremolata	180	4

CHICKEN

RECIPE	PAGE	PORTIONS
Chicken tikka kebabs	76	4
Chicken burgers with tarragon mayonnaise	79	6
Sesame chicken kebabs	80	4
Persian chicken skewers	83	4

SEAFOOD

SOMETHING ON THE SIDE

Some barbecues can be as formal as a dinner party, others as relaxed as a picnic on the beach. Whatever the case, you will need to be prepared—choose the barbecue that suits you best, light the perfect fire and prepare the food to its maximum advantage.

CHOOSING THE BARBECUE

There is a huge range of barbecues on the market these days; each has its own advantages and your decision will depend on how much room you have available, how many you are cooking for and what style of cooking you prefer.

FUEL-BURNING BARBECUES

Brazier

This is the simplest style of fuel-burning barbecue, of which the small, cast-iron hibachi is probably the best known. A brazier consists of a shallow fire-box for burning fuel with a grill on top. Some grills are height-adjustable or can rotate. Braziers are best fitted with a heat-reflecting hood, so that the food is cooked at an even temperature.

Covered kettle barbecue (Weber)

One of the most popular styles of portable barbecue, the kettle barbecue features a close-fitting lid and air vents at top and bottom which allow for greater versatility and accuracy in cooking. Covered barbecues can function as traditional barbecues, ovens or smokers. Kettle barbecues only burn charcoal or heat beads (wood is not recommended) and are relatively small. The standard diameter is 57 cm (22¹/₂ inches) so, if barbecuing for large groups, you may need more than one.

Fixed barbecue

Many gardens contain some sort of fixture for barbecuing. These are relatively simple constructions, usually made from bricks or cement and featuring two grills—the bottom for building the fire, the top for cooking the food. These grills are not generally height-adjustable, so cooking can only be regulated by adjusting the fire, or moving the food away from or towards the fire. Being fixed, these barbecues cannot, of course, be put out of high winds or moved to shelter in the event of rain. Despite this, fixed barbecues are easy to use and maintain and are best if you intend to cook for large numbers.

Gas or Electric Barbecues

Although often more expensive, these barbecues are very simple to use. They do not require an open flame, only connection to their heat source. In most cases, the gas or electricity heats a tray of reusable volcanic rock. Hickory chips can be placed over the rock-bed to give a smoky flavour to the food. Sizes vary, the largest being the trolley-style, which usually features a workbench, reflecting hood and bottom shelf for storage. While small portable gas models, which require only the connection of a gas bottle, are easily manoeuvrable, electric models are confined to areas with mains electricity. Make sure you turn the gas off at the bottle when you have finished cooking to avoid any possibility of a gas leak. Most gas or electric barbecues have temperature controls and accuracy is their primary advantage. Electric models can be fitted with rotisseries or spit turners.

THE FIRE

Fuel

Although traditional, wood is not an ideal fuel for cooking. It can be difficult to light and burns with a flame. Charcoal or heat beads are preferable. They will create a bed of glowing heat which is perfect for cooking. They are readily available in supermarkets or hardware shops and are sometimes known as barbecue briquettes (these should not be confused with heating briquettes, which are not suitable for cooking). Charcoal is wood that has already been burnt down and is the most efficient fuel for barbecuing.

Heat beads don't smell, smoke or flare, but they are difficult to ignite, making firelighters essential. Firelighters have been soaked in kerosene and ignite instantly, but they give off kerosene fumes and food should never be cooked on a barbecue while they are still burning. A couple of firelighters are usually sufficient to light about 20 pieces of charcoal or heat beads. Charcoal and heat beads turn white and have an ash-like coating when ready to use. They burn down to a fine powder, so put a tray underneath for the ash.

A 'normal' fire consists of about 50–60 heat beads or pieces of charcoal and will last for several hours. All recipes in this book can be cooked over a normal fire. The temperature of a fire can always be lowered by damping it with a fine spray of water (a trigger-style plastic spray bottle is ideal). Damping produces steam that will keep the food moist. Do remember that steam burns, so keep your hands well away. Do not damp down a gas barbecue unless it has a metal shield covering the burners.

The best and safest way to increase the heat of a fire is to add more fuel and wait for the fire to develop. Do not fan a fire to increase its heat; this will only produce a flame. Never pour flammable liquids onto a fire.

Smoking

Smoking chips or chunks come from hickory wood, mesquite, dried mallee root, red-gum or acacia trees and are available from barbecue specialists and hardware stores. Their smoke provides an extra and unusual flavour to the cooked food. (Some woods, such as pine, cedar or eucalyptus produce acrid smoke and are unsuitable for cooking. Use only wood sold specifically for smoking.)

Smoking is best done on a covered barbecue (see below) but can also be done on an open fire. Scatter smoking wood throughout the coals. Once the wood is burning, damp down with a little water to create more smoke. Smoking wood is available in chips and chunks; chips burn quickly so should be added towards the end of the cooking process. Chunks should last through the cooking process.

PLANNING YOUR BARBECUE

If you are planning a large get-together with

the barbecue as your means of cookery, it is a good idea to design the whole menu to take full advantage of the barbecue—vegetables, kebabs, breads, even desserts can be cooked or, at least, warmed through easily.

Serve at least one salad or vegetable with the cooked food. Most salad dressings and special sauces can be made in advance and stored in a screw-top jar in the fridge.

Light the fire about an hour before you are planning to use it and don't forget to check the fire occasionally; it can easily go out if unattended.

Assemble all necessary utensils and accessories (for example, tongs, forks, knives, plates and basting brushes) before cooking.

Prepare drinks and dips for when guests arrive, but keep them well away from the fire, both for safety reasons and so the cooking area doesn't get crowded.

Keep a spray bottle of water handy for damping down the fire and a hose or water bottle standing by in case of emergencies. (As a general safety rule, do not attempt to barbecue in strong winds.) A torch may be useful if barbecuing at night. Buy plenty of firelighters and charcoal or heat beads, if that is the fuel you are using.

Always extinguish a fire once you have finished cooking on it. If possible, clean out the barbecue as soon as it has cooled down; brush or scrape grills and flatplates and discard ash and embers.

EQUIPMENT

Again, there is a large selection of equipment for the barbecue and it is up to you how much you buy. However, a few essentials for outdoor cooking are a stiff wire brush or scraper for cleaning away cooked-on food from the grill plate; a pair of long-handled tongs for turning food without singeing the hairs on your arms; a metal slice with a serrated edge for turning

burgers and onions; two pastry brushes for basting; a heatproof mitt for handling metal skewers and hot pans; and a fire blanket or extinguisher.

You could consider a wire fish frame if you like to cook whole fish on the barbecue, or a meat thermometer for testing if large cuts of meat are cooked through.

MARINATING AND BASTING

Marinating
Because most foods are cooked quickly ver high heat on the barbecue, marinating can be used to tenderise meats and fish as well as to add extra flavour. The longer foods are left to marinate, the stronger the flavour will be. Marinating overnight is ideal for beef, lamb and chicken. However, the exception to this rule is fish, which should only be marinated for up to 2 hours or the flesh will start to 'cook' itself in the marinade and become soggy.

To tenderise meat, most marinades will include an acid such as vinegar, citrus juice, wine, or fruit high in enzymes, such as papaya or pine-apple. If so, the food must always be left to marinate in a non-metallic dish, or the acid in the marinade will react with the metal in the dish and affect the food's flavour.

Foods marinated in buttermilk or yoghurt will form a crispy crust—this kind of marinade is perfect for lamb or chicken.

Once the food is marinated, be sure to drain it thoroughly before cooking (unless stated in the recipe). If you add the meat to a flatplate with its marinade, it will stew in the liquid and become tough.

If the marinade is oil- or vinegar-based, you can save it to use as a baste while the meat is cooking. Some marinades can even be put in a pan, brought to the boil and served as a sauce. However, it is very important to remember that marinades have been in contact with raw meat

RARE, MEDIUM OR WELL-DONE MEAT?

Pork and chicken must always be cooked through but with beef and lamb this is a matter of personal taste. Test for 'doneness' by gently pressing the meat with tongs or a flat-bladed knife. If in doubt, remove meat from the barbecue and make a small cut to check its colour. These five classic degrees of 'doneness' have very different appearances and textures.

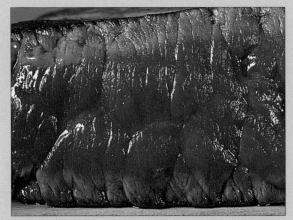

Bleu: Very soft to touch, red-raw inside, outer edge lightly cooked.

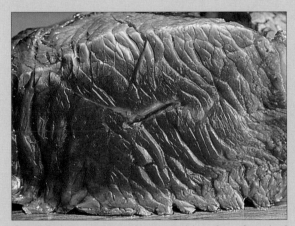

Rare: Soft to touch, red centre, thin edge of cooked meat.

Medium-rare: Springy to touch with moist, pale-red centre.

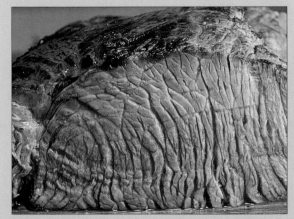

Medium: Firm to touch, pink in centre and crisp, brown edges.

Well-done: Very firm to touch, brown outside and evenly cooked.

and chicken and need to be boiled over high heat before serving. Never be tempted to keep a marinade to re-use—it contains raw meat juices.

Basting

Basting is very useful if you don't have the time to marinate, but would still like to add a little flavour to the food you are barbecuing. While not all foods need to be marinated before barbecuing, all should be basted during cooking, even if it is just with oil to prevent the food sticking to the barbecue. Basting seals moisture and prevents the food from sticking. Baste with olive oil or a reserved marinade, lightly, on both sides. A pastry brush, or clean, unused paintbrush is ideal for this. Do not use a brush with plastic bristles as the plastic may melt onto the food.

COOKING TECHNIQUES

Once food has been marinated, it is ready to cook. Most recipes in this book call for the food to be cooked over a direct flame. Recipes using indirect cooking on covered kettle barbecues can be found on pages 150–61. See the panel on page 7 for instructions on indirect cooking.

Preparation

To use your barbecue efficiently, you are looking for heat rather than flames—always let the flames die down to a bed of red-hot coals before you begin cooking. Once lit, fires should be left to burn for 40–50 minutes before cooking—the heat beads or charcoal will turn white and develop a fine, ash-like coating. (Wood will have a low flame and have begun to char by the time it is ready for cooking.)

Build the fire in the middle of the grate, so that cooked food can be moved to the edge of the grill and kept warm.

To test if the barbecue is ready for cooking, hold the palm of your hand about 10 cm (4 inches) above the grill or plate. If you have to pull it away after 2 seconds, the barbecue is ready.

Direct cooking

As with grilling or frying in the kitchen, the less turning or handling of the food the better. Once the fire is ready, lightly brush the grill or flatplate with oil. Place the food over the hottest part of the fire and sear quickly on both sides—this will help the food retain its moisture by sealing the surface. Once seared, move the food to a cooler part of the grill or flatplate to cook for a few more minutes. Barbecuing is a fast-cooking process so even well-done food will not take very long. The barbecue flatplate is also ideal for stir-frying.

Test meat for doneness by firmly pressing it with tongs or the flat edge of a knife. Meat that is ready to serve should 'give' slightly but not resist pressure too easily. At first, you may find it difficult to judge, but try to resist cutting or stabbing the meat—this not only reduces its succulence by releasing the juices, but the juices can also cause the fire to flare.

While beef and lamb can be cooked from rare to well-done, according to your personal taste (see panel below), pork and chicken should never be served rare. If you are in any doubt whether they are cooked through, remove to a separate plate and make a slight cut in the thickest part of the meat. If the juices do not run clear, return to the heat for further cooking.

Test fish for doneness by gently flaking back the flesh in the thickest part with a fork. Cooked flesh should be white and opaque, but still moist.

INDIRECT COOKING

Indirect cooking on a covered kettle barbecue (weber) roasts or bakes food more slowly than direct cooking. Fragrant wood chips can be added to the coals to give the food flavour.

To prepare for indirect cooking:
1 Remove the lid. Open bottom vent.
2 Put the bottom grill inside the bowl and attach charcoal rails. Heap coals in rails. Put firelighters inside coals.
3 Light fire, leaving lid off. When coals reach fine-ash stage, put a drip-tray or baking dish on bottom grill. Position top grill; add food.

To prepare for smoking:
1 Prepare the barbecue as above.
2 When the coals reach fine-ash stage, add wood chips, fill a drip tray with 1 litre hot water and cover with a lid until fragrant smoke develops.
3 Centre food on top grill and cover.

Heap coals in the charcoal rails and then position two or three firelighters within the coals.

Light the fire and leave the lid off to allow the coals to reach fine-ash stage.

Place a drip tray underneath the top grill when the coals are ready.

For smoking, spoon a generous quantity of smoking wood over the hot coals.

GARLIC DIP WITH CRUDITES

4 cloves garlic, crushed

2 egg yolks

300 ml (10 fl oz) light olive or vegetable oil

1 tablespoon lemon juice

pinch ground white pepper

12 asparagus spears, trimmed

26 radishes, trimmed

$^{1}/_{2}$ telegraph cucumber, seeded, halved and cut into batons

1 head witlof (chicory), leaves separated

1 Place the garlic, egg yolks and a pinch of salt in the bowl of a food processor. Process for 10 seconds.

2 With the motor running, add the oil in a thin, slow stream. The mixture will start to thicken. When this happens you can add the oil a little faster. Process until all the oil is incorporated and the mayonnaise is thick and creamy. Transfer to a bowl and stir in the lemon juice and a pinch of pepper.

3 Bring a saucepan of water to the boil, add the asparagus and cook for 1 minute. Remove and plunge into a bowl of iced water. Arrange the asparagus, radish, cucumber and witlof on a platter and place the garlic dip in a bowl on the platter.

NOTE Should the mayonnaise start to curdle as the oil is added, beat in 1–2 teaspoons boiling water. If this fails, put another egg yolk in a clean bowl and very slowly whisk in the curdled mixture, one drop at a time, then continue as above.

INGREDIENTS

1 kg (2 lb) red capsicums (peppers)
1 teaspoon black peppercorns
2 teaspoons black mustard seeds
2 red onions, thinly sliced
4 cloves garlic, chopped
1^1/$_2$ cups (375 ml/12 fl oz) red wine vinegar
2 apples, peeled, cored and grated
1 teaspoon grated fresh ginger
1 cup (230 g/7^1/$_2$ oz) soft brown sugar

1 Remove the capsicum seeds and membrane and thinly slice. Tie the peppercorns in a piece of muslin and secure with string. Combine the capsicum, peppercorns, mustard seeds, onion, garlic, vinegar, apple and ginger in a large pan. Simmer for 30 minutes until the capsicum is soft.

2 Add the sugar and stir over low heat until completely dissolved. Simmer, stirring occasionally, for 1^1/$_4$ hours, or until the relish has reduced and thickened. Remove the muslin bag.

3 Rinse the jars with boiling water then dry in a warm oven. Spoon the relish into the hot jars and seal. Turn the jars upside down for 2 minutes, then turn them the other way up and leave to cool. Label and date. Leave for a few weeks before using. Will keep in a cool dark place for 1 year. Refrigerate after opening.

TZATZIKI

2 Lebanese cucumbers
400 g (13 oz) Greek-style plain yoghurt
4 cloves garlic, crushed
3 tablespoons finely chopped fresh mint, plus extra to garnish
1 tablespoon lemon juice

1 Cut the cucumbers in half lengthways, scoop out the seeds and discard. Leave the skin on and coarsely grate the cucumber into a small colander. Sprinkle with salt and leave over a large bowl for 15 minutes to drain off any bitter juices.

2 Meanwhile, stir together the yoghurt, crushed garlic, mint and lemon juice.

3 Rinse the cucumber under cold water then, taking small handfuls, squeeze out any excess moisture. Combine the grated cucumber with the yoghurt mixture and season well. Serve immediately with pitta or pide bread or as a sauce with chicken.

INGREDIENTS

400 g (13 oz) Kalamata olives, pitted
2 cloves garlic, crushed
2 anchovy fillets in oil, drained
2 tablespoons capers in brine, rinsed, squeezed dry
2 teaspoons chopped fresh thyme
2 teaspoons Dijon mustard
1 tablespoon lemon juice
3 tablespoons olive oil
1 tablespoon brandy, optional

1 Place the kalamata olives, crushed garlic, anchovies, capers, chopped thyme, Dijon mustard, lemon juice, olive oil and brandy in a food processor and process until smooth. Season with salt and black pepper. Spoon into a clean, warm jar, cover with a layer of olive oil, seal and refrigerate for up to 1 week. Serve as a dip with bruschetta and olives.

NOTE When refrigerated, the olive oil may solidify, turning it opaque white. This is a property of olive oil and will not affect the flavour of the dish. Simply bring to room temperature before serving and the olive oil will return to a liquid state. The word 'tapenade' comes from the French word tapéno, meaning capers. Tapenade is the famous olive, anchovy and caper spread from Provence.

PESTO

50 g (1³/₄ oz) pine nuts
50 g (1³/₄ oz) small fresh basil leaves
2 cloves garlic, crushed
¹/₂ teaspoon sea salt
¹/₂ cup (125 ml/4 fl oz) olive oil
30 g (1 oz) Parmesan, finely grated
20 g (³/₄ oz) pecorino cheese, finely grated

1 Preheat the oven to 180°C (350°F/Gas 4). Spread the pine nuts on a baking tray and bake for 2 minutes, or until lightly golden. Cool.

2 Chop the pine nuts, basil, garlic, salt and oil in a food processor until smooth. Transfer to a bowl and stir in the cheeses. Serve as a dip with bread, crackers or crudités, or as a sauce for barbecued meat, chicken or seafood.

INGREDIENTS

2 eggplants
3 cloves garlic, crushed
$^1/_2$ teaspoon ground cumin
$^1/_3$ cup (80 ml/2$^3/_4$ fl oz) lemon juice
2 tablespoons tahini
pinch cayenne pepper
1$^1/_2$ tablespoons olive oil
1 tablespoon finely chopped fresh flat-leaf parsley
black olives, to garnish

1 Preheat the oven to 200°C (400°F/Gas 6). Pierce the eggplants several times with a fork, then cook over an open flame for about 5 minutes, or until the skin is black and blistering, then place in a roasting tin and bake for 40–45 minutes, or until the eggplants are very soft and wrinkled. Place in a colander over a bowl to drain off any bitter juices and leave to stand for 30 minutes, or until cool.

2 Carefully peel the skin from the eggplant, chop the flesh and place in a food processor with the garlic, cumin, lemon, tahini, cayenne and olive oil. Process until smooth and creamy. Alternatively, use a potato masher or fork. Season with salt and stir in the parsley. Spread onto a flat bowl or plate and garnish with the olives. Serve with flatbread or pide.

NOTE If you prefer, you can simply roast the eggplant in a roasting tin in a 200°C (400°F/Gas 6) oven for 1 hour, or until very soft and wrinkled. Eggplants are also known as aubergines. The name baba ghannouj can be roughly translated as 'poor man's caviar'.

SALMON AND PRAWN KEBABS WITH CHINESE SPICES

4 x 200 g (6^1/$_2$ oz) salmon fillets
36 raw prawns (shrimp), peeled, deveined, tails intact
5 cm (2 inch) piece fresh ginger, finely shredded
^{2}/$_3$ cup (170 ml/5^1/$_2$ fl oz) Chinese rice wine
^{3}/$_4$ cup (185 ml/6 fl oz) kecap manis
^{1}/$_2$ teaspoon five-spice powder
200 g (6^1/$_2$ oz) fresh egg noodles
600 g (1^1/$_4$ lb) baby bok choy, leaves separated

1. Remove the skin and bones from the salmon and cut it into bite-sized cubes (you should have about 36). Thread three cubes of salmon alternately with three prawns onto each skewer. Lay the skewers in a non-metallic dish.

2. Mix together the ginger, rice wine, kecap manis and five-spice powder. Pour over the skewers, then cover and marinate for at least 2 hours. Turn over a few times to ensure even coating.

3. Drain, reserving the marinade. Cook the skewers in batches on a hot, lightly oiled barbecue flatplate or grill for 4–5 minutes each side, or until they are cooked through.

4. Meanwhile, place the noodles in a bowl and cover with boiling water. Leave for 5 minutes, or until tender, then drain and keep warm. Place the reserved marinade in a saucepan and bring to the boil. Reduce the heat, simmer and stir in the bok choy leaves. Cook, covered, for 2 minutes, or until just wilted.

5. Top the noodles with the bok choy, then the kebabs. Spoon on the heated marinade, season and serve.

INGREDIENTS

$^1/_3$ cup (80 ml/2$^3/_4$ fl oz) lemon juice
3 cloves garlic, crushed
1 teaspoon soft brown sugar
$^1/_4$ cup (15 g/$^1/_2$ oz) fresh basil, finely chopped
$^1/_2$ cup (125 ml/4 fl oz) olive oil
4 chicken breast fillets
400 g (13 oz) can cannellini beans, rinsed and drained
100 g (3$^1/_2$ oz) small rocket leaves

1   Whisk together the lemon juice, garlic, sugar, basil and olive oil.

2   Pour a third of the dressing over the chicken to coat. Cook the chicken on a hot, lightly
    oiled barbecue grill or flatplate for 4 minutes on each side, or until cooked through.

3   Meanwhile, combine the beans and rocket with the remaining dressing, toss well and
    season. Slice the chicken and serve over the rocket and beans.

GRILLED HALOUMI AND ROAST VEGETABLE SALAD

4 slender eggplants (aubergines), cut in half and then halved lengthways
1 red capsicum (pepper), halved, thickly sliced
4 small zucchini (courgettes), cut in half and then halved lengthways
$1/3$ cup (80 ml/$2^3/_4$ fl oz) olive oil
2 cloves garlic, crushed
200 g ($6^1/_2$ oz) haloumi cheese, thinly sliced
150 g (5 oz) baby English spinach leaves, trimmed
1 tablespoon balsamic vinegar

1 Preheat the oven to hot 220°C (425°F/Gas 7). Place the vegetables in a large bowl, add $1/4$ cup (60 ml/2 fl oz) of the olive oil and the garlic, season and toss well to combine. Place the vegetables in an ovenproof dish in a single layer. Roast for 20–30 minutes, or until tender and browned around the edges.

2 Meanwhile, cook the haloumi slices on a hot, lightly oiled barbecue grill for 1–2 minutes each side.

3 Top the spinach with the roast vegetables and haloumi. Whisk together the remaining oil and vinegar to make a dressing.

750 g (1¹/₂ lb) mixed mushrooms (such as baby button, oyster, Swiss brown, shiitake and enoki)
2 cloves garlic, finely chopped
¹/₂ teaspoon green peppercorns, crushed
¹/₃ cup (80 ml/2³/₄ fl oz) olive oil
¹/₃ cup (80 ml/2³/₄ fl oz) orange juice
250 g (8 oz) salad leaves, watercress or baby spinach leaves
1 teaspoon finely grated orange rind

1 Trim the mushroom stems and wipe the mushrooms with a damp paper towel. Cut any large mushrooms in half. Mix together the garlic, peppercorns, olive oil and orange juice. Pour over the mushrooms and marinate for about 20 minutes.

2 Arrange the salad leaves in a serving dish.

3 Drain the mushrooms, reserving the marinade. Cook the flat and button mushrooms on a hot, lightly oiled barbecue grill or flatplate for about 2 minutes. Add the softer mushrooms and cook for 1 minute, or until they just soften.

4 Scatter the mushrooms over the salad leaves and drizzle with the marinade. Sprinkle with orange rind and season well.

WARM MARINATED MUSHROOM SALAD

TABBOULEH

3/4 cup (120 g/4 oz) burghul (cracked wheat)
3 ripe tomatoes
1 telegraph cucumber
4 spring onions, sliced
4 cups (120 g/4 oz) chopped fresh flat-leaf parsley
1/2 cup (15 g/1/2 oz) fresh mint, chopped

Dressing
1/3 cup (80 ml/2 3/4 fl oz) lemon juice
3 tablespoons olive oil
1 tablespoon extra virgin olive oil

1 Place the burghul in a bowl, cover with 2 cups (500 ml/16 fl oz) water and leave for 1 hour 30 minutes.

2 Cut the tomatoes in half, squeeze gently to remove the seeds and dice the flesh. Cut the cucumber in half lengthways, remove the seeds with a teaspoon and dice the flesh.

3 To make the dressing, whisk the lemon juice and 1 1/2 teaspoons salt. Slowly whisk in the olive oil and extra virgin olive oil. Season with pepper.

4 Drain the burghul and squeeze out any excess water. Spread on paper towels and leave to dry for 30 minutes. Mix with the tomato, cucumber, spring onion and herbs. Add the dressing and toss together well.

3 large vine-ripened tomatoes
250 g (8 oz) bocconcini or mozzarella
12 fresh basil leaves
3 tablespoons extra virgin olive oil

1 Slice the tomatoes thickly (you will need roughly 12 slices). Slice the bocconcini into about 24 slices.

2 Arrange the tomato slices on a serving plate, alternating them with 2 slices of bocconcini. Place the basil leaves between the bocconcini slices.

3 Drizzle with the oil and season well with salt and ground black pepper.

TOMATO AND BOCCONCINI SALAD

CHARGRILLED VEGETABLES

2 eggplants (aubergines)
900 g (1³/₄ lb) orange sweet potato (kumera)
4 zucchini (courgettes)
2 red capsicums (peppers)
600 g (1¹/₄ lb) button mushrooms
¹/₃ cup (80 ml/2³/₄ fl oz) olive oil

Basil Dressing
¹/₂ cup (125 ml/4 fl oz) olive oil
2 cloves garlic, crushed
2 tablespoons balsamic vinegar
¹/₂ teaspoon sugar
¹/₃ cup (20 g/³/₄ oz) fresh basil leaves

1 Cut the eggplant into 1 cm (¹/₂ inch) thick slices. Place on a wire rack and sprinkle liberally with salt. Leave for 30 minutes, then rinse under cold water and pat dry with paper towels.

2 Cut the sweet potato into 5 mm (¹/₄ inch) slices and the zucchini into 1 cm (¹/₂ inch) slices lengthways. Quarter the capsicums, remove the seeds and membranes and put on a hot, lightly oiled barbecue grill, skin-side-down, until the skin blackens and blisters. Place in a plastic bag and leave to cool. Peel away the skin.

3 Brush the eggplant, sweet potato, zucchini and mushrooms with oil. Cook on a hot, lightly oiled barbecue grill or flatplate in batches until lightly browned and cooked through.

4 To make the basil dressing, put the oil, garlic, vinegar, sugar and basil in a food processor or blender and process until smooth.

5 Toss the vegetables with the basil dressing. Allow to cool, then cover and refrigerate until ready to use. Return to room temperature before serving.

INGREDIENTS

1 large bunch curly endive
$^1/_2$ red oak leaf lettuce
2 red onions
4 slices white or brown (wholemeal) bread
2 large cloves garlic, crushed
60 g (2 oz) butter, softened
30 g (1 oz) feta cheese, mashed
4–6 thin slices prosciutto
1 large avocado

Dressing

2 tablespoons olive oil
3 tablespoons sugar
3 tablespoons spicy tomato sauce
1 tablespoon soy sauce
$^1/_3$ cup (80 ml/2$^3/_4$ fl oz) red wine vinegar

1 Tear the endive and lettuce into pieces. Peel and slice the onions and separate into rings. Toss the endive, lettuce and onion in a salad bowl.

2 Toast the bread on one side only. Mash the garlic, butter and feta cheese into a paste and spread over the untoasted side of the bread. Remove the crusts and toast the buttered side of the bread until crisp and golden. Cut into small cubes.

3 Crisp the prosciutto under a very hot grill for a few seconds. Remove and cut into pieces. Cut the avocado into thin wedges.

4 To make the dressing, whisk the oil, sugar, tomato sauce, soy sauce and vinegar together. Add the prosciutto and avocado to the salad and pour over half the dressing. Arrange the croutons on top and serve the remaining dressing in a jug.

CURLY ENDIVE SALAD WITH CRISP PROSCIUTTO AND GARLIC CROUTONS

WHITE BEAN SALAD WITH TUNA

INGREDIENTS

1 cup (200 g/7 oz) dried cannellini beans or 1 x 425 g (15 oz) can cannellini beans, rinsed and drained well
2 fresh bay leaves
1 large clove garlic, smashed
350 g green beans, trimmed
2 small baby fennel, thinly sliced
$^1/_2$ small red onion, very thinly sliced
1 cup (30 g/1 oz) fresh flat-leaf parsley, roughly chopped
1 tablespoon olive oil
2 fresh tuna steaks (400 g/14 oz)
$^1/_3$ cup (80 ml/2$^3/_4$ fl oz) lemon juice
1 clove garlic, extra, finely chopped
1 small fresh red chilli, seeds removed, finely chopped
1 teaspoon sugar
1 tablespoon lemon zest
$^1/_2$ cup (125 ml/4$^1/_4$ fl oz) extra virgin olive oil

1   Put the beans in a bowl, cover with cold water, allowing room for the beans to expand, and leave for at least 8 hours.

2   Rinse the beans well and transfer them to a saucepan. Cover with cold water, add the torn bay leaves and smashed garlic, and simmer for 20–25 minutes, or until tender. Drain.

3   Cook the green beans in boiling water for 1–2 minutes, or until tender, and refresh under cold water. Mix with the fennel, onion and parsley in a bowl.

4   Brush the oil over the tuna fillets and grill under high heat for 2 minutes on each side or until still pink in the centre. Remove, rest for 2–3 minutes, then cut into 3 cm (1 inch) chunks. Add to the green bean mixture and toss.

5   Mix the lemon juice, garlic, chilli, sugar and lemon zest together. Whisk in the extra virgin olive oil and season with salt and pepper. Toss gently through the salad.

Tomato Relish

400 g (14 oz) can peeled tomatoes

$^2/_3$ cup (170 ml/5$^1/_2$ fl oz) white vinegar

$^1/_2$ cup (125 g/4 oz) sugar

1 clove garlic, finely chopped

2 spring onions, finely chopped

4 sun-dried (sun-blushed) tomatoes, finely chopped

1 small fresh red chilli, finely chopped

$^1/_2$ teaspoon salt

$^1/_2$ teaspoon cracked black pepper

6 large fresh cobs corn

1–2 tablespoons olive or vegetable oil

60 g (2 oz) butter

salt, to serve

1   To make the tomato relish, roughly chop the tomatoes by hand or in a food processor. Put the vinegar and sugar in a pan and stir over heat until the sugar dissolves. Bring to the boil, then reduce the heat and simmer for 2 minutes.

2   Add the tomatoes, garlic, spring onions, sun-dried tomatoes and chilli. Bring to the boil, reduce the heat and simmer, stirring often, for 35 minutes or until thickened. Season, remove from the heat and allow to cool.

3   Brush the corn with oil and cook on a hot, lightly oiled barbecue grill for 10 minutes, or until the corn is soft and flecked with brown in places. Transfer to the flatplate and add a knob of butter and salt to each cob. Serve at once with the relish.

CORN ON THE COB WITH TOMATO RELISH

BARBECUE VEGETABLE AND TOFU KEBABS

500 g (1 lb) firm tofu, cubed
1 red capsicum (pepper), cubed
3 zucchini (courgettes), thickly sliced
4 small onions, cut into quarters
300 g (10 oz) button mushrooms, cut into quarters
$1/2$ cup (125 ml/4 fl oz) tamari
$1/2$ cup (125 ml/4 fl oz) sesame oil
2.5 cm (1 inch) piece ginger, peeled and grated
$1/2$ cup (175 g/6 oz) honey

Peanut sauce
1 tablespoon sesame oil
1 small onion, finely chopped
1 clove garlic, crushed
2 teaspoons chilli paste
1 cup (250 g/8 oz) smooth peanut butter
1 cup (250 ml/8 fl oz) coconut milk
1 tablespoon soft brown sugar
1 tablespoon tamari
1 tablespoon lemon juice
$1/4$ cup (40 g/1$1/4$ oz) peanuts, roasted and chopped
$1/4$ cup (40 g/1$1/4$ oz) sesame seeds, toasted

1 Soak 12 bamboo skewers in water for 2 hours. Thread the tofu, capsicum, zucchini, onions and mushrooms alternately onto the skewers. Lay out in a large flat dish.

2 Combine the tamari, oil, ginger and honey in a non-metallic bowl. Pour over the kebabs. Leave for 30 minutes. Cook on a hot barbecue or in a chargrill pan, basting and turning, for 10–15 minutes, or until tender. Remove and keep warm.

3 To make the peanut sauce, heat the oil in a large frying pan over medium heat and cook the onion, garlic and chilli paste for 1–2 minutes, or until the onion is soft. Reduce the heat, add the peanut butter, coconut milk, sugar, tamari and lemon juice and stir. Bring to the boil, then reduce the heat and simmer for 10 minutes, or until just thick. Stir in the peanuts. If the sauce is too thick, add water. Serve with the kebabs, sprinkled with sesame seeds.

700 g (1 lb 9 oz) rump steak, cut into 2.5 cm (1 inch) cubes

2 small garlic cloves, crushed

3 teaspoons grated ginger

1 tablespoon fish sauce

2 small red chillies, seeded and julienned

Satay sauce

1 tablespoon peanut oil

8 red Asian shallots, finely chopped

8 garlic cloves, crushed

4 small red chillies, finely chopped

1 tablespoon finely chopped ginger

250 g (1 cup) crunchy peanut butter

400 ml (14 fl oz) coconut milk

1 tablespoon soy sauce

60 g ($^1/_3$ cup) grated palm sugar or soft brown sugar

3 tablespoons fish sauce

1 kaffir lime (makrut) leaf

4 tablespoons lime juice

BEEF SATAY

1 Combine the steak with the garlic, ginger and fish sauce and marinate, covered, in the refrigerator for at least 3 hours. Soak eight wooden skewers in cold water for 1 hour.

2 To make the satay sauce, heat the peanut oil in a saucepan over medium heat. Cook the shallots, garlic, chilli and ginger, stirring occasionally, for 5 minutes, or until the shallots are golden. Reduce the heat to low and add the peanut butter, coconut milk, soy sauce, palm sugar, fish sauce, lime leaf and lime juice. Simmer for 10 minutes, or until thickened, then remove the lime leaf.

3 Thread the beef onto the skewers and cook on a barbecue or chargrill pan (griddle) over high heat for 6–8 minutes, or until cooked through, turning halfway through the cooking time. Top with the satay sauce and garnish with the julienned chilli. Serve with rice.

LAMB KEBABS

5 garlic cloves, roughly chopped
5 cm (2 inch) piece of ginger, roughly chopped
3 green chillies, roughly chopped
1 onion, roughly chopped
3 tablespoons thick natural yoghurt
3 tablespoons coriander (cilantro) leaves
$1/2$ teaspoon ground black pepper
500 g (1 lb 2 oz) minced (ground) lamb
red onion rings, to garnish
lemon wedges, to serve

1 Combine the garlic, ginger, chilli, onion, yoghurt and coriander leaves in a food processor to form a thick smooth paste. If you don't have a processor, chop the vegetables more finely and use a mortar and pestle. Add the pepper, season with salt, then mix in the mince. If you are using a mortar and pestle, mix the mince with the paste in a bowl.

2 Divide the meat into 16 portions, about 2 tablespoons each. Shape each portion into an oval patty, cover and chill for 20 minutes.

3 Heat the grill (broiler) to high. Using four metal skewers, thread four meatballs onto each. Grill (broil) for 7 minutes, or until brown on top. Turn over and brown the other side. Check that the meatballs are cooked. Serve with onion rings and lemon wedges.

1 kg (2 lb) minced (ground) beef

1 small onion, finely chopped

2 tablespoons chopped fresh parsley

1 teaspoon dried oregano

1 tablespoon tomato paste (tomato pureé)

70 g (2^1/$_2$ oz) Cheddar cheese

6 bread rolls

Capsicum salsa

2 red capsicums (peppers)

1 ripe tomato, finely chopped

1 small red onion, finely chopped

1 tablespoon olive oil

2 teaspoons red wine vinegar

1 Mix together the mince, onion, herbs and tomato paste with your hands. Divide into six portions and shape into patties. Cut the cheese into small squares. Make a cavity in the top of each patty with your thumb. Place a piece of cheese in the cavity and smooth the mince over to enclose the cheese completely.

2 To make the salsa, quarter the capsicums, remove the seeds and membranes and cook on a hot, lightly oiled barbecue grill, skin-side-down, until the skin blackens and blisters. Place in a plastic bag and leave to cool. Peel away the skin and dice the flesh. Combine with the tomato, onion, olive oil and vinegar and leave for at least 1 hour to let the flavours develop. Serve at room temperature.

3 Cook the patties on a hot, lightly oiled barbecue grill or flatplate for 4–5 minutes each side, turning once. Serve in rolls with salad leaves and the capsicum salsa.

CHEESEBURGERS WITH CAPSICUM SALSA

INGREDIENTS

350 g (11 oz) calamari (squid) tubes, cleaned
4 cloves garlic, chopped
2 tablespoons olive oil
2 tablespoons finely chopped fresh parsley
1 large tomato, peeled, seeded and finely chopped
$^1/_4$ cup (25 g/$^3/_4$ oz) grated Parmesan

1 Cut the calamari tubes in half lengthways, wash and pat dry. Lay them flat, with the soft, fleshy side facing upwards, and cut into rectangular pieces, about 6 x 2.5 cm (2$^1/_2$ x 1 inch). Finely honeycomb by scoring the fleshy side with diagonal strips, one way and then the other, to create a diamond pattern.

2 Mix the garlic, oil, half the parsley, salt and pepper in a bowl. Add the calamari and refrigerate for at least 10 minutes.

3 Cook on a very hot, lightly oiled barbecue flatplate in 2 batches, tossing regularly, until they just turn white (take care never to overcook calamari or it can become tough). Add the chopped tomato and toss through to just heat.

4 Arrange the calamari on a plate and scatter with the Parmesan and remaining parsley.

NOTE This dish will serve four as a starter and two as a main course.

INGREDIENTS

800 g (1 lb 12 oz) rump steak

2 teaspoons ground cumin

1 teaspoon ground oregano

1 teaspoon paprika

2 tablespoons Worcestershire sauce

1 tablespoon soy sauce

3 garlic cloves

60 ml ($^1/_4$ cup) lime juice

1 large onion, thinly sliced

1 red capsicum (pepper), cut into 5 mm ($^1/_4$ inch) strips

1 green capsicum (pepper), cut into 5 mm ($^1/_4$ inch) strips

1 tablespoon olive oil

8 flour tortillas

1 ripe avocado, diced

2 ripe Roma (plum) tomatoes, diced

60 g ($^1/_2$ cup) grated Cheddar cheese

90 g ($^1/_3$ cup) sour cream

1 Trim the steak of any fat and give it a good pounding with a meat mallet on both sides. Mix the cumin, oregano, paprika, Worcestershire sauce, soy sauce, garlic and lime juice in a shallow, non-metallic dish and add the beef. Turn until well coated in the marinade, then cover and refrigerate for at least 4 hours, or overnight.

2 Drain the steak, reserving the marinade, and pat it dry with paper towels. Simmer the marinade in a small saucepan over medium heat for 5 minutes, or until it is reduced by about half, and keep it warm.

3 Preheat a barbecue to high direct heat. Toss the onion and capsicum with the oil then spread them across the flat plate, turning every so often, for 10 minutes, or until cooked through and caramelized. While the vegetables are cooking, grill the steak on the chargrill plate for 3 minutes each side, or until cooked to your liking. Remove it from the heat and let it rest, covered, for 5 minutes. Thinly slice the steak and arrange it on a plate with the onion and capsicum strips and serve with the tortillas, avocado, tomato, cheese, sour cream and marinade sauce. Let everyone fill their own tortillas.

BEEF KEBABS WITH MINT YOGHURT DRESSING

500 g (1 lb) lean beef fillet, cubed
$1/2$ cup (125 ml/4 fl oz) olive oil
$1/3$ cup (80 ml/$2^3/4$ fl oz) lemon juice
1 tablespoon chopped fresh rosemary
1 red onion, cut into wedges
200 g ($6^1/2$ oz) slender eggplants (aubergines), sliced

Mint yoghurt dressing
1 cup (250 g/8 oz) plain yoghurt
1 clove garlic, crushed
1 small Lebanese cucumber, grated
2 tablespoons chopped fresh mint

1 Leave 8 wooden skewers to soak in cold water to prevent scorching. Put the beef in a non-metallic bowl, combine the olive oil, lemon juice and rosemary and pour over the beef. Cover and refrigerate for 2 hours.

2 To make the mint yoghurt dressing, mix together the yoghurt, garlic, cucumber and mint and season with salt and pepper.

3 Drain the beef and thread onto the skewers, alternating pieces of beef with the onion wedges and slices of eggplant.

4 Cook the kebabs on a hot, lightly oiled barbecue grill or flatplate, turning often, for 5–10 minutes, or until the beef is cooked through and tender. Serve with the dressing.

INGREDIENTS

1 kg (2 lb) swordfish, skin removed, cut into four 5 cm (2 inch) pieces
3 lemons
4 tablespoons olive oil
1 small onion, chopped
3 cloves garlic, chopped
2 tablespoons chopped capers
2 tablespoons chopped pitted Kalamata olives
$1/3$ cup (35 g/1 oz) finely grated Parmesan
$1^1/2$ cups (120 g/4 oz) fresh breadcrumbs
2 tablespoons chopped fresh parsley
1 egg, lightly beaten
24 fresh bay leaves
2 small white onions, quartered and separated into pieces
2 tablespoons lemon juice, extra

1 Cut each swordfish piece horizontally into four slices to give you 16 slices. Place each piece between two pieces of plastic wrap and roll gently with a rolling pin to flatten without tearing. Cut each piece in half to give 32 pieces.

2 Peel the lemons with a vegetable peeler. Cut the peel into 24 even pieces. Squeeze the lemons to give 3 tablespoons of juice.

3 Heat 2 tablespoons olive oil in a pan, add the onion and garlic, and cook over medium heat for 2 minutes. Place in a bowl with the capers, olives, Parmesan, breadcrumbs and parsley. Season, add the egg and mix to bind.

4 Divide the stuffing among the fish pieces and, with oiled hands, roll up to form parcels. Thread four rolls onto each of eight skewers alternating with the bay leaves, lemon peel and onion.

5 Mix the remaining oil with the lemon juice in a small bowl. Cook the skewers on a hot barbecue flatplate for 3–4 minutes each side, basting with the oil and lemon mixture. Serve with a little extra lemon juice drizzled over the top.

VEGETARIAN BURGERS WITH CORIANDER GARLIC CREAM

1 cup (250 g/8 oz) red lentils
1 tablespoon oil
2 onions, sliced
1 tablespoon tandoori mix powder
425 g (14 oz) can chickpeas, drained
1 tablespoon grated fresh ginger
1 egg
3 tablespoons chopped fresh parsley
2 tablespoons chopped fresh coriander (cilantro)
2¹/₄ cups (180 g/6 oz) fresh breadcrumbs
plain (all-purpose) flour, for dusting

Coriander garlic cream
¹/₂ cup (125 g/4 oz) sour cream
¹/₂ cup (125 ml/4 fl oz) cream
1 clove garlic, crushed
2 tablespoons chopped fresh coriander (cilantro)
2 tablespoons chopped fresh parsley

1 Simmer the lentils in a large pan of water for 8 minutes or until tender. Drain well. Heat the oil in a pan and cook the onion until tender. Add the tandoori mix and stir until fragrant.

2 Put the chickpeas, half the lentils, the ginger, egg and onion mixture in a food processor. Process for 20 seconds or until smooth. Transfer to a bowl. Stir in the remaining lentils, parsley, coriander and breadcrumbs.

3 Divide into 10 portions and shape into burgers. (If the mixture is too soft, refrigerate for 15 minutes to firm.) Toss the burgers in flour and place on a hot, lightly oiled barbecue grill or flatplate. Cook for 3–4 minutes each side or until browned.

4 For the coriander garlic cream, mix together the sour cream, cream, garlic and herbs. Serve with the burgers.

NOTE The coriander garlic cream is also delicious with chicken or fish burgers.

1 kg (2 lb) boned leg lamb, trimmed and cut into small cubes
3 tablespoons olive oil
2 teaspoons finely grated lemon rind
4 tablespoons lemon juice
2 teaspoons dried oregano
$^1/_2$ cup (125 ml/4 fl oz) dry white wine
2 large cloves garlic, finely chopped
2 fresh bay leaves
1 cup (250 g/8 oz) Greek-style plain yoghurt
2 cloves garlic, crushed, extra

1 Place the lamb in a non-metallic bowl with 2 tablespoons of the olive oil, the lemon rind and juice, oregano, wine, garlic and bay leaves. Season with black pepper and toss to coat. Cover and refrigerate overnight.

2 Place the yoghurt and extra garlic in a bowl, mix together well and leave for 30 minutes. If using wooden skewers, soak for 30 minutes beforehand to prevent scorching.

3 Drain the lamb and pat dry. Thread onto 8 skewers and cook on a hot barbecue flatplate, brushing with the remaining oil, for 7–8 minutes, or until brown on the outside and still a little rare in the middle. Drizzle with the garlic yoghurt and serve with warm pitta bread.

LAMB SOUVLAKI

TUNA SKEWERS WITH MOROCCAN SPICES AND CHERMOULA

800 g (1 lb 10 oz) tuna steaks, cut into cubes
2 tablespoons olive oil
$^1/_2$ teaspoon ground cumin
2 teaspoons grated lemon rind

Chermoula
3 teaspoons ground cumin
$^1/_2$ teaspoon ground coriander (cilantro)
2 teaspoons paprika
pinch of cayenne pepper
4 garlic cloves, crushed
$^1/_2$ cup (15 g/$^1/_2$ oz) chopped fresh flat-leaf parsley
$^1/_2$ cup (30 g/1 oz) chopped fresh coriander (cilantro)
4 tablespoons lemon juice
$^1/_2$ cup (125 ml/4 fl oz) olive oil

1 If using wooden skewers, soak for 30 minutes beforehand to prevent scorching. Place the tuna in a shallow non-metallic dish. Combine the olive oil, ground cumin and lemon rind and pour over the tuna. Toss to coat and leave to marinate for 10 minutes.

2 To make the chermoula, place the cumin, coriander, paprika and cayenne in a frying pan and cook over medium heat for 30 seconds, or until fragrant. Combine with the remaining ingredients and leave for the flavours to develop.

3 Thread the tuna onto the skewers. Cook on a hot, lightly oiled barbecue grill or flatplate until cooked to your taste (about 1 minute on each side for rare and 2 minutes for medium). Serve on couscous with the chermoula drizzled over the skewers.

INGREDIENTS

1 large red capsicum (pepper), cubed
12 button mushrooms, halved
6 pickling onions, quartered
3 zucchini (courgettes), cut into chunks
450 g (14 oz) firm tofu, cubed
$^{1}/_{2}$ cup (125 ml/4 fl oz) light olive oil
3 tablespoons light soy sauce
2 cloves garlic, crushed
2 teaspoons grated fresh ginger

Miso pesto
$^{1}/_{2}$ cup (90 g/3 oz) unsalted roasted peanuts
2 cups (60 g/2 oz) firmly packed fresh coriander (cilantro) leaves
2 tablespoons white miso paste
2 cloves garlic
100 ml (3$^{1}/_{2}$ oz) olive oil

1   If using wooden skewers, soak them in water for 30 minutes to prevent scorching. Thread the vegetables and tofu alternately onto 12 skewers, then place in a large non-metallic dish.

2   Mix together the olive oil, soy sauce, garlic and ginger, then pour half over the kebabs. Cover and leave to marinate for 1 hour.

3   To make the miso pesto, finely chop the peanuts, coriander leaves, miso paste and garlic in a food processor. Slowly add the olive oil while the machine is still running and blend to a smooth paste.

4   Cook the kebabs on a hot, lightly oiled barbecue flatplate or grill, turning and brushing with the remaining marinade, for 4–6 minutes, or until the edges are slightly brown. Serve with the miso pesto.

INGREDIENTS

500 g (1 lb 2 oz) minced (ground) beef
6 red Asian shallots, finely chopped
25 g ($^1/_4$ cup) crisp fried onion flakes (see note)
3 garlic cloves, finely chopped
2 long red chillies, seeded and finely chopped
20 g ($^1/_3$ cup) finely chopped coriander (cilantro) leaves (include some stems)
2–2$^1/_2$ tablespoons chilli garlic sauce (see note)
1 egg, lightly beaten
160 g (2 cups/5$^1/_2$ oz) fresh breadcrumbs
olive oil, for brushing
1 loaf Turkish bread, cut into 4 pieces, or 4 round Turkish rolls
100 g (3 handfuls) mignonette or green oak lettuce leaves

1   To make the burgers, put the beef, shallots, onion flakes, garlic, chilli, coriander, chilli garlic sauce, egg, breadcrumbs and 1$^1/_2$ teaspoons of salt in a large bowl, and knead well with your hands until the ingredients are thoroughly combined. Cover the bowl and refrigerate for 2 hours.

2   Using wet hands, divide the beef mixture into four equal portions, roll each portion into a ball, then flatten it slightly to form patties. Preheat the chargrill plate to medium direct heat. Brush the patties lightly with oil and grill them for 5–6 minutes, then flip them over and cook for another 5–6 minutes, or until they are well browned and cooked through. A few minutes before the patties are done, toast the bread, cut-side down, on the chargrill plate for 1–2 minutes, or until it is marked and golden.

3   Divide the lettuce among four of the toasted bread slices. Add a patty, season the burgers with salt and pepper, then top with the remaining toasted bread.

NOTE   Crisp fried onion flakes and chilli garlic sauce are available from Asian grocery stores.

400 g (13 oz) lamb leg steaks
2 teaspoons finely grated lemon rind
3 teaspoons finely chopped fresh oregano
2 cloves garlic, finely chopped
2 tablespoons olive oil
1 red onion, thinly sliced
4 small pitta breads
$^1/_2$ cup (125 g/4 oz) hummus
$^1/_2$ cup (125 g/4 oz) plain yoghurt
1 small Lebanese cucumber, thinly sliced
1 small red chilli, seeds removed, finely chopped
snow pea (mangetout) sprouts

1 Trim the lamb of excess fat and cut into thin strips. Mix together the lemon rind, oregano, garlic, olive oil and some cracked black pepper in a non-metallic bowl. Add the lamb and refrigerate for 15 minutes.

2 Cook the lamb and onion on a very hot, lightly oiled barbecue flatplate for 2–3 minutes, turning to brown the meat quickly and soften the onion. Remove from the plate and keep warm. Place the pitta breads on the flatplate and warm both sides.

3 Spread each round of bread with a little of the hummus and yoghurt. Add the barbecued lamb and onion and scatter with the cucumber, chilli and a few snow pea sprouts.

SPICY SEAFOOD SKEWERS

Spice paste

2 large red chillies, seeded and chopped

1 clove garlic, chopped

2 spring onions, finely chopped

1 teaspoon grated fresh ginger

1 tablespoon grated fresh turmeric

1 small tomato, peeled and seeded

$1/2$ teaspoon coriander (cilantro) seeds

2 tablespoons chopped roasted peanuts

$1/2$ teaspoon dried shrimp paste

2 teaspoons vegetable oil

1 tablespoon tamarind concentrate

1 tablespoon finely chopped lemon grass

350 g (11 oz) skinned boneless snapper fillet

350 g (11 oz) raw prawns (shrimp), peeled and deveined

1 egg, lightly beaten

2 cups (120 g/4 oz) flaked coconut

4 kaffir lime (makrut) leaves, shredded

2 tablespoons brown sugar

$3/4$ cup (185 g/6 oz) whole egg mayonnaise

3 teaspoons grated lime rind

1 tablespoon chopped fresh coriander (cilantro)

1 Soak 6 thick wooden skewers in water for 30 minutes.

2 To make the paste, coarsely grind the chilli, garlic, spring onion, ginger, turmeric, tomato, coriander, peanuts and shrimp paste in a food processor. Heat the oil in a frying pan and cook the chilli mixture, tamarind and lemon grass for 5 minutes over medium heat, stirring frequently, until golden. Put aside to cool before using.

3 Finely mince the fish and prawns in a food processor. Add the egg, coconut, kaffir lime leaves, sugar and spice paste. Season well with salt and pepper. Process until well combined.

4 Using wet hands, shape $1/4$ cup of mixture around each skewer, then cook on a hot, lightly oiled barbecue flatplate or grill for 8–10 minutes, turning often, until golden. Mix the mayonnaise, lime rind and coriander in a bowl and serve with the skewers.

INGREDIENTS

5 thin zucchini (courgettes), cut into 2 cm ($^3/_4$ inch) cubes
5 slender eggplants (aubergines), cut into 2 cm ($^3/_4$ inch) cubes
12 button mushrooms, halved
2 red capsicums (peppers), cut into 2 cm ($^3/_4$ inch) cubes
250 g (9 oz) kefalotyri cheese, cut into 2 cm ($^3/_4$ inch) thick pieces
80 ml ($^1/_3$ cup) lemon juice
2 garlic cloves, finely chopped
5 tablespoons finely chopped basil
145 ml (5 fl oz) extra virgin olive oil
185 g (1 cup) couscous
1 teaspoon grated lemon zest
lemon wedges, to serve

1 Using 12 metallic skewers, thread alternate pieces of vegetables and kefalotyri, starting and finishing with capsicum and using two pieces of kefalotyri per skewer. Place in a large non-metallic dish. Combine the lemon juice, garlic, 4 tablespoons of basil and 125 ml ($^1/_2$ cup) of oil in a non-metallic bowl. Season. Pour two-thirds of the marinade over the skewers, reserving the remainder. Turn the skewers to coat evenly, cover with plastic wrap and marinate for at least 5 minutes.

2 Put the couscous, zest and 375 ml (1$^1/_2$ cups) boiling water in a large heatproof bowl. Stand for 5 minutes, or until the water has been absorbed. Add the remaining oil and basil, then fluff with a fork to separate the grains.

3 Meanwhile, heat a barbecue plate to medium–high. Cook the skewers, brushing often with the leftover marinade, for 4–5 minutes each side, or until the vegetables are cooked and the cheese browns.

4 Divide the couscous and skewers among four serving plates. Season, then drizzle with the reserved marinade. Serve immediately with lemon wedges.

INGREDIENTS

10 chicken thigh fillets, cubed
1 red onion, cut into wedges
3 tablespoons tikka paste
$^1/_2$ cup (125 ml/4 fl oz) coconut milk
2 tablespoons lemon juice

1   Soak 8 skewers in water to prevent scorching. Thread 2 pieces of chicken and a wedge of onion alternately along each skewer. Place the skewers in a shallow, non-metallic dish.

2   Combine the tikka paste, coconut milk and lemon juice in a jar with a lid. Season and shake well to combine. Pour the mixture over the skewers and marinate for at least 2 hours, or overnight if time permits.

3   Cook the skewers on a hot, lightly oiled barbecue grill or flatplate for 4 minutes on each side, or until the chicken is cooked through. Put any leftover marinade in a small pan and bring to the boil. Serve as a sauce with the tikka kebabs.

1 kg (2 lb) minced (ground) chicken
1 small onion, finely chopped
2 teaspoons finely grated lemon rind
2 tablespoons sour cream
1 cup (90 g/3 oz) fresh breadcrumbs
6 onion bread rolls

Tarragon mayonnaise
1 egg yolk
1 tablespoon tarragon vinegar
$^1/_2$ teaspoon French mustard
1 cup (250 ml/8 fl oz) olive oil

1 Mix together the mince, onion, rind, sour cream and breadcrumbs with your hands. Divide into six portions and shape into burgers.

2 To make the mayonnaise, put the yolk, half the vinegar and the mustard in a small bowl. Whisk for 1 minute until light and creamy. Add the oil about 1 teaspoon at a time, whisking constantly until the mixture thickens. Increase the flow of oil to a thin stream and continue whisking until it has all been incorporated. Stir in the remaining vinegar and season well with salt and white pepper.

3 Cook the burgers on a hot, lightly oiled barbecue flatplate or grill for 7 minutes each side, turning once. Serve on a roll with the mayonnaise.

CHICKEN BURGERS WITH TARRAGON MAYONNAISE

INGREDIENTS

3 tablespoons oil
2 tablespoons soy sauce
2 tablespoons honey
1 tablespoon grated fresh ginger
1 tablespoon sesame oil
4 large chicken breast fillets, cubed
8 spring onions, cut into short lengths
1 tablespoon toasted sesame seeds

1 Soak 12 wooden skewers in water to prevent scorching. To make the marinade, whisk together the oil, soy sauce, honey, ginger and sesame oil. Thread the chicken and spring onion onto the skewers and put in a non-metallic dish. Add the marinade, cover and refrigerate for at least 2 hours.

2 Place the skewers on a hot, lightly oiled barbecue flatplate or grill and baste with the remaining marinade. Cook for 4 minutes on each side, or until the chicken is cooked through. Sprinkle with the sesame seeds.

2 teaspoons ground cardamom
$^1/_2$ teaspoon ground turmeric
1 teaspoon ground allspice
4 cloves garlic, crushed
3 tablespoons lemon juice
3 tablespoons olive oil
4 large chicken thigh fillets, excess fat removed
lemon wedges, to serve
plain yoghurt, to serve

1   Soak 8 wooden skewers in water to prevent scorching. To make the marinade, whisk
    together the cardamom, turmeric, allspice, garlic, lemon juice and oil. Season with salt and
    ground black pepper.

2   Cut each chicken thigh fillet into 3–4 cm (1–1$^1/_2$ inch) cubes. Toss the cubes in the spice
    marinade. Thread the chicken onto skewers and place on a tray. Cover and refrigerate
    overnight.

3   Cook the skewers on a hot, lightly oiled barbecue grill or flatplate for 4 minutes on each
    side, or until the chicken is cooked through. Serve with lemon wedges and plain yoghurt.

PERSIAN CHICKEN SKEWERS

INGREDIENTS

32 chicken tenderloins
24 cherry tomatoes
6 cap mushrooms, cut into quarters
2 cloves garlic, crushed
rind of 1 lemon, grated
2 tablespoons lemon juice
2 tablespoons olive oil
1 tablespoon fresh oregano leaves, chopped

1 Soak 8 wooden skewers in water to prevent scorching. Thread a piece of chicken onto each skewer, followed by a tomato, then a piece of mushroom. Repeat three times for each skewer. Put the skewers in a shallow, non-metallic dish.

2 Combine the garlic, lemon rind, lemon juice, olive oil and chopped oregano, pour over the skewers and toss well. Marinate for at least 2 hours, or overnight if time permits.

3 Cook the skewers on a hot, lightly oiled barbecue grill or flatplate for 4 minutes on each side, basting occasionally, until the chicken is cooked and the tomatoes have shrivelled slightly.

4 chicken thigh fillets (400 g/13 oz)
1¹/₂ tablespoons soft brown sugar
1¹/₂ tablespoons lime juice
2 teaspoons green curry paste
18 kaffir lime (makrut) leaves
2 stems lemon grass

Mango salsa
1 small mango, finely diced
1 teaspoon grated lime rind
2 teaspoons lime juice
1 teaspoon soft brown sugar
¹/₂ teaspoon fish sauce

1 Discard any excess fat from the chicken and cut in half lengthways. Combine the sugar, lime juice, curry paste and 2 of the kaffir lime leaves, shredded, in a bowl. Add the chicken and mix well. Cover and refrigerate for several hours or overnight.

2 Trim the lemon grass to 20 cm (8 inches), leaving the root end intact. Cut each stem lengthways into four pieces. Cut a slit in each of the remaining lime leaves and thread one onto each piece of lemon grass. Cut two slits in each piece of chicken and thread onto the lemon grass, followed by another lime leaf. Pan-fry or barbecue until cooked through.

3 To make the mango salsa, put the mango, lime rind, juice, sugar and fish sauce in a bowl and stir gently to combine. Serve with the lemon grass skewers.

LEMON GRASS AND CHICKEN SKEWERS

LAMB SOUVLAKI ROLL

500 g (1 lb) lamb backstrap or loin fillet
100 ml (3^1/$_2$ fl oz) olive oil
3 tablespoons dry white wine
1 tablespoon fresh oregano
3 tablespoons roughly chopped fresh basil
3 cloves garlic, crushed
2 bay leaves, crushed
2^1/$_2$ tablespoons lemon juice
1 large loaf Turkish bread
1 cup (250 g/8 oz) baba ganouj
1 tablespoon roughly chopped fresh parsley

1 Place the lamb in a shallow non-metallic dish. Mix together the oil, wine, oregano, basil, garlic, bay leaves and 2 tablespoons of the lemon juice and pour over the lamb, turning to coat well. Cover with plastic wrap and marinate for 4 hours.

2 Cook the lamb on a hot, lightly oiled barbecue grill or flatplate for 6–8 minutes, or until seared but still pink in the centre. Remove from the heat and rest for 10 minutes, then cut into slices.

3 Split the Turkish bread lengthways and spread the bottom thickly with the baba ganouj. Top with the lamb, sprinkle with the parsley and remaining lemon juice, then season with salt and pepper. Replace the top of the loaf, then cut into quarters to serve.

8 chicken drumsticks, scored
1 tablespoon mustard powder
2 tablespoons tomato sauce
1 tablespoon sweet mango chutney
1 teaspoon Worcestershire sauce
1 tablespoon Dijon mustard
$\frac{1}{4}$ cup (30 g/1 oz) raisins
1 tablespoon oil

1 Toss the chicken in the mustard powder and season.

2 Combine the tomato sauce, chutney, Worcestershire sauce, mustard, raisins and oil. Spoon over the chicken and toss well. Marinate for at least 2 hours, turning once.

3 Cook the chicken on a hot, lightly oiled barbecue flatplate for about 20 minutes, or until cooked through.

DRUMSTICKS IN TOMATO AND MANGO CHUTNEY

CORIANDER PRAWNS

8 very large raw prawns (shrimp)
1 tablespoon sweet chilli sauce
1 teaspoon ground coriander (cilantro)
125 ml ($\frac{1}{2}$ cup) olive oil
80 ml ($\frac{1}{3}$ cup) lime juice
3 garlic cloves, crushed
1 tomato, peeled, seeded and chopped
2 tablespoons roughly chopped coriander (cilantro)

1 Remove the heads from the prawns and, with a sharp knife, cut the prawns in half lengthways, leaving the tails attached. Pull out each dark vein.

2 Mix together the sweet chilli sauce and ground coriander with half the olive oil, half the lime juice and half the garlic. Add the prawns, toss to coat, then cover and marinate in the fridge for 30 minutes.

3 Meanwhile, to make the dressing, mix the remaining olive oil, lime juice and garlic in a bowl with the chopped tomato and coriander.

4 Drain the prawns, reserving the marinade and cook, cut-side down, on a hot, lightly oiled barbecue grill or flat plate for 1–2 minutes each side, or until cooked through, brushing occasionally with the marinade. Spoon a little of the dressing over the prawns and season well with salt and pepper before serving.

3 tablespoons Thai red curry paste
1 cup (250 ml/8 fl oz) coconut milk
2 tablespoons lime juice
4 tablespoons finely chopped fresh coriander (cilantro) leaves
12 chicken drumsticks, scored
2 bunches (1 kg/2 lb) baby bok choy
2 tablespoons soy sauce
1 tablespoon oil

1 Combine the curry paste, coconut milk, lime juice and coriander. Place the chicken in a shallow, non-metallic dish and pour on the marinade. Cover and marinate in the fridge for at least 2 hours.

2 Cook the chicken on a lightly oiled barbecue grill for 50–60 minutes, or until cooked through.

3 Trim the bok choy and combine with the soy sauce and oil, then cook on the barbecue or in a wok for 3–4 minutes, or until just wilted. Serve the chicken on a bed of bok choy.

THAI DRUMSTICKS

HERB BURGERS

750 g (1¹/₂ lb) minced (ground) beef or lamb
2 tablespoons chopped fresh basil
1 tablespoon chopped fresh chives
1 tablespoon chopped fresh rosemary
1 tablespoon chopped fresh thyme
2 tablespoons lemon juice
1 cup (90 g/3 oz) fresh breadcrumbs
1 egg
2 long crusty bread sticks
lettuce leaves
2 tomatoes, sliced
tomato sauce

1 Combine the mince with the herbs, juice, breadcrumbs, egg and season well with salt and pepper. Mix well with your hands. Divide the mixture into eight portions and shape into thick rectangular patties.

2 Place the burgers on a hot, lightly oiled barbecue grill or flatplate. Cook for 5–10 minutes each side until well browned and just cooked through.

3 Cut the bread sticks in half and sandwich with the burgers, lettuce, tomato and tomato sauce.

INGREDIENTS

3 tablespoons yellow or red miso paste
2 tablespoons sugar
3 tablespoons sake
2 tablespoons mirin
1 kg (2 lb) chicken thighs, boned
1 cucumber
2 spring onions, sliced

1 If using wooden skewers, soak them in water for 30 minutes to prevent scorching. Place the miso, sugar, sake and mirin in a small saucepan over medium heat and cook, stirring well, for 2 minutes, or until the sauce is smooth and the sugar has dissolved completely.

2 Cut the chicken into cubes. Seed the cucumber and cut into small batons. Thread the chicken, cucumber and spring onion alternately onto the skewers—you should have about three pieces of each per skewer.

3 Cook on a hot, lightly oiled barbecue flatplate, turning occasionally, for 10 minutes, or until the chicken is almost cooked. Brush with the miso sauce and continue cooking, then turn and brush the other side. Repeat once or twice until the chicken and vegetables are cooked.

SPICY BURGERS WITH AVOCADO SALSA

INGREDIENTS

1 kg (2 lb) minced (ground) beef
1 small onion, finely chopped
3 teaspoons chopped chilli
1 teaspoon ground cumin
2 tablespoons tomato paste (tomato pureé)
2 tablespoons chopped fresh coriander (cilantro)
6 bread rolls

Avocado Salsa

1 avocado
2 tablespoons lime juice
1 small tomato, chopped
125 g (4 oz) can corn kernels, drained

1 With your hands, mix together the mince, onion, chilli, cumin, tomato paste and coriander. Divide into six portions and shape into burgers.

2 Cook on a hot, lightly oiled grill or flatplate for 4–5 minutes each side.

3 To make the salsa, dice the avocado and toss with lime juice. Add the tomato and corn and toss lightly. Sandwich the burgers in the bread rolls and serve with the salsa.

INGREDIENTS

750 g (1¹/₂ lb) swordfish fillets, cut into cubes

Marinade
¹/₂ cup (125 ml/4 fl oz) teriyaki sauce
¹/₄ cup (60 ml/2 fl oz) pineapple juice
2 tablespoons honey
1 tablespoon grated fresh ginger
2 cloves garlic, crushed
1 teaspoon sesame oil

Salsa
1 red onion, chopped
2 teaspoons sugar
2 tablespoons lime juice
1 firm mango, diced
1 cup (150 g/5 oz) diced pineapple
1 kiwi fruit, diced
2 small red chillies, seeded and finely chopped
2 tablespoons finely chopped fresh coriander
    (cilantro) leaves

1 Soak 8 wooden skewers in water to prevent scorching. Place the cubes of fish in a non-metallic bowl. Combine the marinade ingredients, pour over the fish and stir to coat. Cover and refrigerate for 30 minutes.

2 Thread the fish onto the skewers, keeping the marinade.

3 To make the salsa, put the onion in a bowl and sprinkle with sugar. Add the other ingredients and mix together gently.

4 Cook the skewers on a hot, lightly oiled barbecue flatplate or grill for 6–8 minutes, turning often and basting with the reserved marinade. Serve with the salsa.

NOTE You should only marinate fish for 30 minutes; any longer and the fish flesh will begin to 'cook' in the marinade and break down.

TERIYAKI FISH WITH MANGO SALSA

INGREDIENTS

4 garlic cloves, crushed
2 egg yolks
250 ml (1 cup) light olive oil
3 tablespoons chopped flat-leaf (Italian) parsley
1 tablespoon chopped dill
2 teaspoons Dijon mustard
1 tablespoon lemon juice
1 tablespoon red wine vinegar
1 tablespoon baby capers in brine, drained
4 anchovy fillets in oil, drained
4 x 150 g (5$^1/_2$ oz) tuna steaks
2 tablespoons olive oil
2 red onions, thinly sliced
4 large round bread rolls, halved and buttered
100 g (3$^1/_2$ oz) mixed lettuce leaves

1   Put the garlic and egg yolks in a food processor and process them together for 10 seconds. With the motor running, add the oil in a very thin, slow stream. When the mixture starts to thicken start pouring the oil a little faster until all of the oil has been added and the mixture is thick and creamy. Add the parsley, dill, mustard, lemon juice, vinegar, capers and anchovies, and process until the mixture is smooth. Refrigerate the mayonnaise until you need it.

2   Preheat the chargrill plate to high direct heat. Brush the tuna steaks with 1 tablespoon of olive oil and cook them for 2 minutes on each side, or until they are almost cooked through. Add the remaining olive oil to the onion, toss to separate and coat the rings, and cook on the flat plate for 2 minutes, or until the onion is soft and caramelized. Toast the rolls, buttered-side down, on the chargrill plate for 1 minute, or until they are marked and golden.

3   Put some lettuce, a tuna steak, some of the onion and a dollop of herbed mayonnaise on one half of each roll. Season with salt and pepper and top with the other half of the roll.

INGREDIENTS

4 sirloin steaks
3 tablespoons seasoned cracked pepper

Horseradish Sauce
2 tablespoons brandy
3 tablespoons beef stock
4 tablespoons cream
1 tablespoon horseradish cream
$1/2$ teaspoon sugar

1   Coat the steaks on both sides with pepper, pressing it into the meat. Cook on a hot, lightly oiled barbecue grill or flatplate for 5–10 minutes, until cooked to your taste.

2   To make the sauce, put the brandy and stock in a pan. Bring to the boil, then reduce the heat. Stir in the cream, horseradish and sugar and heat through. Serve with the steaks.

PEPPER STEAKS WITH HORSERADISH SAUCE

INGREDIENTS

Salsa verde

1 cup (20 g/³/₄ oz) fresh parsley leaves
1 cup (50 g/1³/₄ oz) fresh basil leaves
1 cup (20 g/³/₄ oz) fresh mint leaves
¹/₂ cup (30 g/1 oz) fresh dill
2 tablespoons capers
1–2 cloves garlic
1 tablespoon caster sugar
1 teaspoon grated lemon rind
1 tablespoon lemon juice
1 slice white bread
2–3 anchovy fillets
¹/₃ cup (80 ml/2³/₄ fl oz) olive oil

Polenta wedges

2 cups (500 ml/16 fl oz) chicken stock
1 cup (150 g/5 oz) polenta (cornmeal)
50 g (1³/₄ oz) butter
¹/₂ cup (125 ml/4 fl oz) cream

12 lamb cutlets, trimmed

1   To make the salsa verde, chop the herbs, capers, garlic, sugar, lemon rind, juice, bread and anchovies in a food processor. With the motor running, add the oil in a thin stream and blend until smooth.

2   To make the polenta, heat the stock until boiling. Add the polenta, stirring over low heat for 20 minutes until it leaves the side of the pan. Stir in the butter and cream and season. Grease a deep 23 cm (9 inch) round cake tin, spoon in the polenta and smooth the top. Set in the fridge for 20 minutes.

3   Turn out the polenta, cut into wedges and brush with melted butter. Cook on a hot, lightly oiled barbecue grill or flatplate for 2–3 minutes each side, or until brown.

4   Cook the lamb for 2 minutes on each side, or until cooked through but still just pink inside.

INGREDIENTS

100 g (3$^1/_2$ oz) butter, softened

50 g ($^1/_3$ cup) semi-dried (sun-blushed) tomatoes, finely chopped

2 tablespoons baby capers in brine, drained and crushed

1$^1/_2$ tablespoons shredded basil leaves

4 garlic cloves, crushed

60 ml ($^1/_4$ cup) extra virgin olive oil

300 g (10$^1/_2$ oz) slender asparagus spears, trimmed

4 swordfish steaks

1 Put the butter in a bowl with the tomato, capers, basil and two cloves of crushed garlic, and mash it all together. Shape the flavoured butter into a log, then wrap it in baking paper and twist the ends to close them off. Refrigerate until the butter is firm, then cut it into 1 cm ($^1/_2$ inch) slices and leave it, covered, at room temperature until needed.

2 Mix 2 tablespoons of the oil and the remaining garlic in a small bowl. Toss the asparagus spears with the oil until they are well coated, season them with salt and pepper, and leave for 30 minutes.

3 Preheat a ridged barbecue grill plate to high direct heat. Brush the swordfish steaks with the remaining oil and cook them for 2–3 minutes on each side or until they are just cooked through. Don't overcook the fish as residual heat will continue to coo the meat after it has been removed from the barbecue. Put a piece of the tomato butter on top of each steak as soon as it comes off the barbecue and season to taste. Cook the asparagus on the chargrill plate, turning it regularly, for 2–3 minutes, or until it is just tender. Serve the asparagus immediately with the fish.

INGREDIENTS

300 g lamb backstraps or fillets
1¹/₂ tablespoons black pepper
3 vine-ripened tomatoes, cut into 8 wedges
2 Lebanese cucumbers, sliced
150 g (5 oz) lemon and garlic marinated Kalamata olives, drained (reserving 1¹/₂ tablespoons oil)
100 g (3¹/₂ oz) Greek feta cheese, cubed
³/₄ teaspoon dried oregano
1 tablespoon lemon juice
1 tablespoon extra virgin olive oil

1   Roll the backstraps in the pepper, pressing the pepper on with your fingers. Cover and refrigerate for 15 minutes.

2   Place the tomato, cucumber, olives, feta and ¹/₂ teaspoon of the dried oregano in a bowl.

3   Heat a chargrill pan or barbecue plate, brush with oil and when very hot, cook the lamb for 2–3 minutes on each side, or until cooked to your liking. Keep warm.

4   Whisk the lemon juice, extra virgin olive oil, reserved Kalamata oil and the remaining dried oregano together well. Season. Pour half the dressing over the salad, toss together and arrange on a serving platter.

5   Cut the lamb on the diagonal into 1 cm thick slices and arrange on top of the salad. Pour the remaining dressing on top and serve.

INGREDIENTS

Salsa verde
1 clove garlic
2 cups (60 g/2 oz) firmly packed fresh flat-leaf parsley
$^1/_3$ cup (80 ml/2$^3/_4$ fl oz) extra virgin olive oil
3 tablespoons chopped fresh dill
1$^1/_2$ tablespoons Dijon mustard
1 tablespoon sherry vinegar
1 tablespoon baby capers, drained

6 large chicken breast fillets

1   Place all the ingredients for the salsa verde in a food processor or blender and process until almost smooth.

2   Cook the chicken fillets on a very hot, lightly oiled barbecue grill or flatplate for 4–5 minutes each side, or until cooked through.

3   Cut each chicken fillet into three on the diagonal and arrange on serving plates. Top with a spoonful of salsa verde and season to taste.

TANDOORI CHICKEN

INGREDIENTS

$^1/_2$ cup (125 g/4 oz) Greek-style plain yoghurt
2 tablespoons tandoori paste
2 cloves garlic, crushed
2 tablespoons lime juice
1$^1/_2$ teaspoons garam masala
2 tablespoons finely chopped fresh coriander (cilantro) leaves
6 chicken thigh fillets

1 Combine the yoghurt, tandoori paste, garlic, lime juice, garam masala and coriander in a bowl and mix well.

2 Add the chicken, coat well, cover and refrigerate for at least 1 hour.

3 Cook the chicken on a hot, lightly oiled barbecue grill or flatplate for 5 minutes on each side, basting with the remaining marinade, until golden and cooked through. Serve with cucumber raita and naan bread.

INGREDIENTS

750 g (1 lb 10 oz) small, firm white fish
2 teaspoons green peppercorns, finely crushed
2 teaspoons chopped red chilli
3 teaspoons fish sauce
2 teaspoons oil
1 tablespoon oil, extra
2 onions, finely sliced
4 cm (1¹/₂ inch) piece fresh ginger, peeled and thinly sliced
3 garlic cloves, finely sliced
2 teaspoons sugar
4 spring onions (scallions), cut into short lengths, then
  finely shredded

Lemon and garlic dipping sauce

3 tablespoons lemon juice
2 tablespoons fish sauce
1 tablespoon sugar
2 small red chillies, chopped
3 garlic cloves, crushed

1 Cut 2 diagonal slashes in the thickest part of the fish on both sides. In a food processor or mortar and pestle, grind the peppercorns, chilli and fish sauce to a paste and brush over the fish. Leave for 20 minutes.

2 To make the dipping sauce, mix together all the ingredients.

3 Cook the fish on a hot, lightly oiled barbecue grill or flat plate for 8 minutes on each side, or until the flesh flakes easily when tested.

4 While the fish is cooking, heat the extra oil in a pan and stir the onion over medium heat, until golden. Add the ginger, garlic and sugar and cook for 3 minutes. Place the fish on a serving plate, top with the onion mixture and sprinkle with spring onion. Serve with the dipping sauce.

CHERMOULA CHICKEN

$^1/_2$ cup (15 g/$^1/_2$ oz) firmly packed fresh flat-leaf parsley

$^1/_4$ cup (7 g/$^1/_4$ oz) firmly packed fresh coriander (cilantro) leaves

2 cloves garlic, roughly chopped

3 tablespoons lemon juice

1 tablespoon chopped preserved lemon

3 teaspoons ground cumin

$^1/_2$ cup (125 ml/4 fl oz) olive oil

4 chicken breast fillets, flattened (see note)

1 Mix the parsley, coriander, garlic, lemon juice, preserved lemon and cumin in a food processor until well combined. With the motor running, gradually add the oil in a thin stream until smooth. Season well.

2 Place the chicken in a shallow, non-metallic dish and pour over the marinade. Marinate for at least 2 hours.

3 Grease four sheets of foil and place a chicken breast in the centre of each. Spoon any extra marinade over the chicken. Fold the foil over to seal. Cook the parcels on a hot, lightly oiled barbecue flatplate for 10–12 minutes without turning, until cooked through. Remove from the foil and slice.

NOTE To flatten chicken fillets, place between two pieces of plastic wrap and hit with a meat mallet or the palm of your hand.

INGREDIENTS

1¹/₂ tablespoons onion powder
1¹/₂ tablespoons garlic powder
2 teaspoons paprika
1 teaspoon white pepper
2 teaspoons dried thyme
¹/₂–1 teaspoon chilli powder (see note)
8 chicken drumsticks, scored

1 Combine the herbs, spices and 1 teaspoon salt in a plastic bag. Place the drumsticks in the bag and shake until all the pieces are coated. Leave the chicken in the fridge for at least 30 minutes to allow the flavours to develop, or overnight if time permits.

2 Cook the chicken on a lightly oiled barbecue grill for 55–60 minutes, or until slightly blackened and cooked through. Brush lightly with some oil to prevent drying out during cooking.

NOTE Chilli powder is very hot, so only use ¹/₂ teaspoon if you prefer a milder flavour.

BLACKENED CAJUN SPICED CHICKEN

ASIAN BARBECUED CHICKEN

2 cloves garlic, finely chopped
$1/4$ cup (60 ml/2 fl oz) hoisin sauce
3 teaspoons light soy sauce
3 teaspoons honey
2 tablespoons tomato sauce or sweet chilli sauce
1 teaspoon sesame oil
2 spring onions, finely sliced
1.5 kg (3 lb) chicken wings

1 To make the marinade, mix together the garlic, hoisin sauce, soy, honey, tomato sauce, sesame oil and spring onion.

2 Put the chicken wings in a shallow, non-metallic dish, add the marinade, cover and leave in the fridge for at least 2 hours.

3 Cook the chicken on a hot, lightly oiled barbecue grill, turning once, for 20–25 minutes, or until cooked and golden brown. Baste with the marinade during cooking. Heat any remaining marinade in a pan until boiling and serve as a sauce.

INGREDIENTS

6 bird's eye chillies, with seeds left in, finely chopped
1 teaspoon coarse salt
$^1/_2$ cup (125 ml/4 fl oz) olive oil
$^3/_4$ cup (185 ml/6 fl oz) cider vinegar
1 clove garlic, crushed
4 chicken Maryland pieces (see note)
lemon wedges, to serve

1 Combine the chilli, salt, olive oil, vinegar and garlic in a screw-top jar. Seal and shake well to combine.

2 Place the chicken pieces in a shallow, non-metallic dish and pour on the marinade. Cover and marinate for at least 1 hour.

3 Cook the chicken on a hot, lightly oiled barbecue grill or flatplate, basting regularly with the marinade, for 50–60 minutes, or until the chicken is cooked through and the skin begins to crisp. Serve with lemon wedges.

NOTE Marylands are the drumstick and thigh pieces of the chicken. Any chicken cut that is still on the bone can be used in this recipe. Piri-piri is also excellent for barbecuing prawns. Seed the chillies for a milder tasting dish.

PIRI-PIRI CHICKEN

INGREDIENTS

1 onion, grated
4 cloves garlic, chopped
5 cm (2 inch) piece of fresh ginger, grated
3 stems lemon grass (white part only), chopped
2 teaspoons ground or grated fresh turmeric
1 teaspoon shrimp paste
$^1/_3$ cup (80 ml/2$^3/_4$ fl oz) vegetable oil
$^1/_4$ teaspoon salt
4 medium calamari (squid) tubes
2 thick white boneless fish fillets
8 raw king prawns (jumbo shrimp)
banana leaves, for serving
2 limes, cut into wedges

1 Combine the onion, garlic, ginger, lemon grass, turmeric, shrimp paste, oil and salt in a small food processor. Process in short bursts until the mixture forms a paste.

2 Cut the calamari in half lengthways and lay it on the bench with the soft inside facing up. Score a very fine honeycomb pattern into the soft side, taking care not to cut all the way through, and then cut into large pieces. Wash all the seafood under cold running water and pat dry with paper towels. Brush the seafood lightly with the spice paste. Place the seafood on a tray, cover and refrigerate for 15 minutes.

3 Lightly oil a barbecue hotplate and heat. When the plate is hot, arrange the fish fillets and prawns side by side on the plate. Cook for about 3 minutes on each side, turning them once only, or until the fish flesh is just firm and the prawns turn bright pink to orange. Add the calamari pieces and cook for about 2 minutes or until the flesh turns white and rolls up—take care not to overcook the seafood.

4 Arrange the seafood on a platter lined with the banana leaves, add the lime wedges and serve immediately, garnished with strips of lime rind and some fresh mint, if you like.

NOTE Banana leaves are available from speciality fruit and vegetable shops. Alternatively, make friends with someone who has a banana tree.

INGREDIENTS

3 tablespoons chopped fresh dill

2 tablespoons chopped fresh rosemary

3 tablespoons coarsely chopped fresh flat-leaf parsley

2 teaspoons thyme leaves

6 teaspoons crushed green peppercorns

$^1/_3$ cup (80 ml/2$^3/_4$ fl oz) lemon juice

1 lemon

4 whole fresh trout

$^1/_3$ cup (80 ml/2$^3/_4$ fl oz) dry white wine

Horseradish Cream

1 tablespoon horseradish cream

$^1/_2$ cup (125 g/4 oz) sour cream

2 tablespoons cream

Lemon Sauce

2 egg yolks

150 g (5 oz) butter, melted

3-4 tablespoons lemon juice

1 Lightly grease 4 large sheets of foil, each double-thickness. Mix together the herbs, peppercorns, juice and salt and pepper in a bowl. Cut the lemon into 8 slices, cut each slice in half. Place 2 lemon pieces in each fish cavity. Spoon the herb mixture into the fish cavities.

2 Place each fish on a piece of foil and sprinkle each with 1 tablespoon of wine. Seal the fish in foil to form neat parcels. Cook on a hot barbecue flatplate or grill for 10–15 minutes or until the fish is just cooked through and can be gently flaked with a fork. Leave the fish to stand, still wrapped in foil, for 5 minutes, before serving.

3 To make the horseradish cream, mix together all the ingredients and then season well.

4 To make the lemon sauce, process the yolks in a food processor for 20 seconds or until blended. With the motor running, add the butter slowly in a thin, steady stream. Continue processing until all butter has been added and the sauce is thick and creamy. Add the juice and season with salt and pepper.

INGREDIENTS

Basil aïoli
1 garlic clove
15 g ('/₄ cup) torn basil leaves
1 egg yolk
125 ml ('/₂ cup) olive oil
2 teaspoons lemon juice

2 large red capsicums (peppers), quartered, core and seeds removed
1 eggplant (aubergine), cut in 5 mm ('/₄ inch) thick rounds
1 orange sweet potato (kumera), peeled and cut on the diagonal into 5 mm ('/₄ inch) thick rounds
3 zucchini (courgettes), sliced lengthways into 5 mm ('/₄ inch) thick slices
2 red onions, cut into 1 cm ('/₂ inch) thick rounds
80 ml ('/₃ cup) olive oil
1 loaf Turkish bread, split and cut into 4 equal pieces

1 To make the basil aïoli, put the garlic, basil and egg yolk in a food processor and blend until smooth. With the motor running, gradually add the oil in a thin stream until the mixture thickens. Stir in the lemon juice and season to taste. Cover and refrigerate until you are ready to dish up.

2 Preheat a barbecue chargrill plate to medium direct heat. Put the capsicum, skin-side down, around the cool edge of the grill and cook it for 8–10 minutes or until the skin has softened and is blistering.

3 Meanwhile, brush the eggplant, sweet potato, zucchini and onion slices on both sides with olive oil and season them lightly. Cook the vegetables in batches on the middle of the chargrill for 5–8 minutes, or until they are cooked through but still firm. As the vegetable pieces cook, put them on a tray in a single layer to prevent them from steaming, then grill the Turkish bread on both sides until it is lightly marked and toasted.

4 Spread both cut sides of the bread with 1 tablespoon of basil aïoli and pile on some of the chargrilled vegetables. Top with the remaining toast and serve immediately.

INGREDIENTS

2 garlic cloves, crushed
1 tablespoon fish sauce
2 tablespoons lemon juice
1 tablespoon grated fresh ginger
2 tablespoons sweet chilli sauce
2 tablespoons chopped fresh coriander (cilantro)
1 tablespoon rice wine vinegar
2 tablespoons white wine
600 g (1 1/4 lb) whole snapper, cleaned and scaled
2 spring onions, cut into julienne strips

1 Mix together the garlic, fish sauce, lemon juice, ginger, chilli sauce, coriander, rice wine vinegar and wine.

2 Place the snapper on a large piece of double-thickness foil. Pour the marinade over the fish and sprinkle with the spring onion.

3 Wrap the fish in the foil to make a parcel. Cook over medium heat on a barbecue grill or flatplate for 20–30 minutes, or until the flesh flakes easily when tested with a fork.

6 pork butterfly steaks
250 ml (1 cup) ginger wine
150 g (¹/₂ cup) orange marmalade
2 tablespoons oil
1 tablespoon grated fresh ginger

1 Trim the pork steak of excess fat and sinew. Mix together the wine, marmalade, oil and ginger. Place the steaks in a shallow non-metallic dish and add the marinade. Store, covered with plastic wrap, in the fridge for at least 3 hours, turning occasionally. Drain, reserving the marinade.

2 Cook the pork on a hot, lightly oiled barbecue flat plate or grill for 5 minutes each side or until tender, turning once.

3 While the meat is cooking, place the reserved marinade in a small pan. Bring to the boil, reduce the heat and simmer for 5 minutes, or until the marinade has reduced and thickened slightly. Pour over the pork.

GINGER-ORANGE PORK

INGREDIENTS

Marinade
$1/2$ cup (125 ml/4 fl oz) olive oil
$1/3$ cup (80 ml/$2^3/_4$ fl oz) lemon juice
2 tablespoons wholegrain mustard
2 tablespoons honey
2 tablespoons chopped fresh dill

16–20 raw king prawns (jumbo shrimp)

Dill Mayonnaise
$3/4$ cup (185 g/6 oz) mayonnaise
2 tablespoons chopped fresh dill
$1^1/2$ tablespoons lemon juice
1 gherkin, finely chopped
1 teaspoon chopped capers
1 clove garlic, crushed

1   To make the marinade, combine the olive oil, lemon juice, mustard, honey and dill, pour over the unpeeled prawns and coat well. Cover and refrigerate for at least 2 hours, turning occasionally.

2   To make the dill mayonnaise, whisk together the mayonnaise, dill, lemon juice, gherkin, capers and garlic. Cover and refrigerate.

3   Cook the drained prawns on a hot, lightly oiled barbecue grill or flatplate in batches for 4 minutes, turning frequently until pink and cooked through. Serve with the mayonnaise.

INGREDIENTS

4 garlic cloves, crushed
1 tablespoon grated ginger
1 teaspoon oil
1 teaspoon sambal oelek
2 teaspoons ground coriander (cilantro)
2 teaspoons ground cumin
2 tablespoons soy sauce
2 teaspoons sesame oil
2 tablespoons sweet chilli sauce
2 tablespoons lemon juice
12 lamb cutlets

1 Combine the garlic, ginger, oil, sambal oelek, coriander, cumin, soy sauce, sesame oil, sweet chilli sauce and lemon juice in a bowl. Season with salt and cracked black pepper.

2 Place the cutlets in a non-metallic dish and pour on the marinade, coating all sides. Leave to marinate for 20 minutes.

3 Cook the cutlets on a very hot chargrill pan (griddle) or barbecue for 3 minutes each side, or until cooked to your liking. Serve with steamed rice.

CHILLI LAMB CUTLETS

CAJUN PRAWNS WITH SALSA

Cajun spice mix

1 tablespoon garlic powder
1 tablespoon onion powder
2 teaspoons dried thyme
2 teaspoons ground white pepper
1¹/₂ teaspoons cayenne pepper
¹/₂ teaspoon dried oregano

Tomato salsa

4 Roma (plum) tomatoes, seeded and chopped
1 Lebanese (short) cucumber, peeled, seeded, chopped
2 tablespoons finely diced red onion
2 tablespoons chopped coriander (cilantro)
1 tablespoon chopped flat-leaf (Italian) parsley
1 garlic clove, crushed
2 tablespoons olive oil
1 tablespoon lime juice

1.25 kg (2 lb 12 oz) large raw prawns (shrimp)
100 g (3¹/₂ oz) butter, melted
60 g (2¹/₄ oz) watercress, washed and picked over
4 spring onions (scallions), chopped
lemon wedges, to serve

1 Combine all the ingredients for the Cajun spice mix with 2 teaspoons cracked black pepper.

2 To make the tomato salsa, combine the tomato, cucumber, onion, coriander and parsley in a bowl. Mix the garlic, oil and lime juice together and season well. Add to the bowl and toss together.

3 Peel and devein the prawns, leaving the tails intact. Brush the prawns with the butter and sprinkle generously with the spice mix. Cook on a barbecue hotplate or under a hot grill (broiler), turning once, for 2–3 minutes each side, or until a crust forms and the prawns are pink and cooked.

4 Lay some watercress on serving plates, then spoon the salsa over the leaves. Arrange the prawns on top and sprinkle with some chopped spring onion. Serve with lemon wedges on the side.

TUNA WITH CAPONATA

Caponata
500 g (1 lb) ripe tomatoes
750 g (1¹/₂ lb) eggplant (aubergine), diced
¹/₃ cup (80 ml/2³/₄ fl oz) olive oil
2 tablespoons olive oil, extra
1 onion, chopped
3 celery sticks, chopped
2 tablespoons drained capers
¹/₂ cup (90 g/3 oz) green olives, pitted
1 tablespoon sugar
¹/₂ cup (125 ml/4 fl oz) red wine vinegar

6 x 200 g (6¹/₂ oz) tuna steaks

1 To make the caponata, score a cross in the base of each tomato. Place in a bowl of boiling water for 1 minute, then plunge into cold water and peel the skin away from the cross. Cut into small cubes.

2 Sprinkle the eggplant with salt and leave for 1 hour. Place in a colander, rinse under cold running water and pat dry. Heat the oil in a frying pan and cook the eggplant, in batches, for 4–5 minutes, or until golden and soft. Remove from the pan.

3 Heat the extra oil in the pan, add the onion and celery, and cook for 3–4 minutes, or until golden. Reduce the heat to low, add the tomato and simmer for 15 minutes, stirring occasionally. Stir in the capers, olives, sugar and vinegar, season and simmer, stirring occasionally, for 10 minutes, or until slightly reduced. Stir in the eggplant. Allow to cool.

4 Cook the tuna on a hot, lightly oiled barbecue grill or flatplate for 2–3 minutes each side, or until cooked to your liking. Serve immediately with the caponata.

INGREDIENTS

1 kg (2 lb) calamari (squid)
1 cup (250 ml/8 fl oz) olive oil
2 tablespoons lemon juice
2 cloves garlic, crushed
2 tablespoons chopped fresh oregano
2 tablespoons chopped fresh flat-leaf parsley
lemon wedges, to serve

Salsa verde
2 anchovy fillets, drained
1 tablespoon capers
1 clove garlic, crushed
2 tablespoons chopped fresh flat-leaf parsley
2 tablespoons olive oil

1 To clean the calamari, hold onto the hood and gently pull the tentacles away from the head. Cut out the beak and discard with any intestines still attached to the tentacles. Rinse the tentacles in cold running water, pat dry and cut into 5 cm (2 inch) lengths. Place in a bowl. Clean out the hood cavity and remove the transparent backbone. Under cold running water, pull away the skin, rinse and dry well. Cut into rings and place in the bowl with the tentacles. Add the oil, lemon juice, garlic and oregano and toss to coat. Refrigerate for 30 minutes.

2 To make the salsa verde, crush the anchovy fillets in a mortar and pestle. Rinse and chop the capers very finely and mix with the anchovies. Add the garlic and parsley, then slowly stir in the olive oil. Season and mix well.

3 Drain the calamari and cook on a hot, lightly oiled barbecue grill or flatplate in batches for 1–2 minutes each side, basting with the marinade. To serve, sprinkle the calamari with salt, pepper and fresh parsley, and serve with the salsa verde and lemon wedges.

GARLIC SCALLOPS WITH ANGEL HAIR PASTA

20 large scallops with corals
250 g (8 oz) angel hair pasta
150 ml (5 fl oz) extra virgin olive oil
2 cloves garlic, finely chopped
$^1/_4$ cup (60 ml/2 fl oz) white wine
1 tablespoon lemon juice
100 g (3$^1/_2$ oz) baby rocket leaves
30 g (1 oz) chopped fresh coriander (cilantro)

1 Pull or trim any veins, membrane or hard white muscle from the scallops. Pat dry with paper towels. Cook the pasta in boiling water until al dente. Drain and toss with 1 tablespoon oil to keep it from sticking.

2 Meanwhile, heat 1 tablespoon oil in a frying pan, add the garlic and cook for a few seconds. Add the combined wine and lemon juice and remove from the heat.

3 Season the scallops with salt and pepper and cook on a hot, lightly oiled barbecue grill or flatplate for 1 minute each side, or until just cooked. Gently reheat the garlic mixture, add the rocket and stir over medium heat for 1–2 minutes, or until wilted. Toss through the pasta with the remaining oil, coriander and scallops.

8 (800 g) large raw king prawns (jumbo shrimp)
$\frac{1}{3}$ cup (80 ml/2$\frac{3}{4}$ fl oz) olive oil
3 cloves garlic, crushed
1 tablespoon sweet chilli sauce
2 tablespoons lime juice
$\frac{1}{4}$ cup (60 ml/2 fl oz) olive oil, extra
2 tablespoons lime juice, extra

1 Remove the heads from the prawns and, using a sharp knife, cut through the centre of the prawns lengthways to form two halves, leaving the tails and shells intact.

2 Place the olive oil, 2 crushed garlic cloves, sweet chilli sauce and lime juice in a shallow, non-metallic dish and mix together well. Add the prawns, toss to coat and marinate for 30 minutes. Meanwhile, combine the extra oil and lime juice and remaining garlic to make a dressing.

3 Drain the prawns and cook on a hot barbecue grill or flatplate, cut-side-down first, for 1–2 minutes each side, brushing with the leftover marinade. Serve the prawns with the dressing spooned over the top of them.

JUMBO PRAWNS

INGREDIENTS

800 g (1 lb 12 oz) lamb loin
60 ml ($\frac{1}{4}$ cup) hoisin sauce
2 tablespoons soy sauce
2 garlic cloves, bruised
1 tablespoon grated fresh ginger
2 teaspoons olive oil
16 spring onions (scallions), trimmed to 18 cm (7 inches) long
40 g ($\frac{1}{4}$ cup) chopped toasted peanuts

1 Trim the lamb of any excess fat and sinew. Combine the hoisin sauce, soy sauce, garlic, ginger and 1 teaspoon of the oil in a shallow dish, add the lamb and turn it so that it is well coated in the marinade. Cover the dish and refrigerate for 4 hours or overnight.

2 Toss the trimmed spring onions with the remaining oil and season them well. Remove the lamb from the marinade, season the meat and pour the marinade into a small saucepan. Simmer the marinade for 5 minutes, or until it is slightly reduced. Preheat a chargrill plate to medium direct heat. Cook the lamb for 5–6 minutes on each side, or until it is cooked to your liking, brushing it frequently with the reduced marinade, then let it rest, covered, for 3 minutes. Grill the spring onions for 1–2 minutes, or until they are tender, but still firm.

3 Cut the lamb across the grain into 2 cm ($\frac{3}{4}$ inch) thick slices, and arrange it on a serving plate. Drizzle any juices that have been released during resting over the lamb and sprinkle it with the toasted peanuts. Serve with the spring onions.

INGREDIENTS

¹/₂ cup (125 ml/4 fl oz) teriyaki marinade
¹/₂ teaspoon five-spice powder
1 tablespoon grated fresh ginger
3 tuna steaks, each cut into 4 strips
¹/₄ cup (60 g/2 oz) mayonnaise
1 teaspoon wasabi paste
2 tablespoons pickled ginger, to serve

1 Combine the teriyaki marinade, five-spice powder and ginger. Place the tuna in a non-metallic dish, pour over the marinade, cover and leave to marinate for 10 minutes. Drain and discard the marinade.

2 Cook the tuna, in batches if necessary, on a very hot, lightly oiled barbecue flatplate for 1–2 minutes each side, or until cooked to your taste. Cooking time will vary depending on the thickness of the tuna steaks.

3 Mix together the mayonnaise and wasabi paste and serve with the tuna steaks, garnished with pickled ginger.

TERIYAKI TUNA WITH WASABI MAYONNAISE AND PICKLED GINGER

SWEET CHILLI OCTOPUS

INGREDIENTS

1.5 kg (3 lb) baby octopus
1 cup (250 ml/8 fl oz) sweet chilli sauce
$^1/_3$ cup (80 ml/2$^3/_4$ fl oz) lime juice
$^1/_3$ cup (80 ml/2$^3/_4$ fl oz) fish sauce
$^1/_3$ cup (60 g/2 oz) soft brown sugar
lime wedges, to serve

1   Cut off the octopus heads, below the eyes, with a sharp knife. Discard the heads and guts. Push the beaks out with your index finger, remove and discard. Wash the octopus thoroughly under running water and drain on crumpled paper towels. If the octopus tentacles are large, cut into quarters.

2   Mix together the sweet chilli sauce, lime juice, fish sauce and sugar.

3   Cook the octopus on a very hot, lightly oiled barbecue grill or flatplate, turning often, for 3–4 minutes, or until it just changes colour. Brush with a quarter of the sauce during cooking. Do not overcook the octopus or it will toughen. Serve immediately with the remaining sauce and lime wedges.

INGREDIENTS

500 g (1 lb) raw king prawns (jumbo shrimp)

Marinade
2 tablespoons lemon juice
2 tablespoons sesame oil
2 cloves garlic, crushed
2 teaspoons grated fresh ginger

1 Peel and devein the prawns, leaving the tails intact. Make a cut in the prawn body, slicing three-quarters of the way through the flesh from head to tail. Put the prawns in a non-metallic dish or bowl.

2 To make the marinade, mix together the lemon juice, oil, garlic and ginger and pour over the prawns. Cover and refrigerate for 2 hours.

3 Cook the prawns on a hot, lightly oiled barbecue flatplate for 3–5 minutes or until pink and cooked through. Brush frequently with the marinade while cooking and then serve immediately.

GARLIC PRAWNS

INGREDIENTS

Garlic mash
1 kg (2 lb 4 oz) floury (starchy) potatoes, cut into chunks
6–8 garlic cloves, peeled
80 ml ($^1/_3$ cup) milk
60 ml ($^1/_4$ cup) olive oil

Salsa
1 tablespoon olive oil
2 French shallots, finely chopped
200 g (7 oz) green olives, pitted and quartered lengthways
35 g ($^1/_4$ cup) currants, soaked in warm water for 10 minutes
1 tablespoon baby capers, rinsed and squeezed dry
1 tablespoon sherry vinegar
2 tablespoons shredded mint leaves

4 tuna steaks (about 150 g/5$^1/_2$ oz each)
olive oil, for brushing
sea salt

1 Boil the potato chunks and garlic for 10–15 minutes, or until tender. Drain them, then return the pan to the heat, shaking it to evaporate any excess water. Remove the pan from the heat and mash the potato and garlic until smooth, then stir in the milk and olive oil, and season with salt and freshly ground black pepper.

2 To make the salsa, heat the oil in a frying pan over medium heat. Cook the shallots for 2–4 minutes, or until they are softened, but not browned, then add the olives, drained currants and capers. Cook for 2 minutes, stirring continuously, then add the vinegar and cook for 2 minutes, or until the liquid is reduced by about half. Remove the pan from the heat and keep the salsa warm until you're ready to dish up.

3 Preheat a barbecue chargrill plate to medium–high direct heat. Brush the tuna steaks with olive oil, season them well with sea salt and freshly ground black pepper, and grill for 2–3 minutes each side for medium–rare, or until they are cooked to your liking. Stir the mint into the salsa and serve it immediately with the garlic mash and tuna.

1 kg (2 lb) chicken thigh fillets
2 tablespoons lime juice
$^1/_2$ cup (125 ml/4 fl oz) sweet chilli sauce
$^1/_4$ cup (60 ml/2 fl oz) kecap manis (see note)

1 Trim any excess fat from the chicken thigh fillets and cut them in half. Transfer to a shallow non-metal dish.

2 Place the lime juice, sweet chilli sauce and kecap manis in a bowl and whisk to combine.

3 Pour the marinade over the chicken, cover and refrigerate for 2 hours.

4 Chargrill for 10–15 minutes, turning once, or until the chicken is tender and cooked through and the marinade has caramelized.

NOTE Kecap manis (ketjap manis) is a thick Indonesian sauce, similar to—but sweeter than—soy sauce, and is generally flavoured with garlic and star anise. Store in a cool, dry place and refrigerate after opening. If not available, use soy sauce sweetened with a little soft brown sugar.

SWEET CHILLI CHICKEN

CHILLI PORK RIBS

1 kg (2 lb 4 oz) pork spareribs
125 g (4¹/₂ oz) tin puréed tomatoes
2 tablespoons honey
2 tablespoons chilli sauce
2 tablespoons hoisin sauce
2 tablespoons lime juice
2 garlic cloves, crushed
1 tablespoon oil

1 Cut each rib into thirds, then lay them in a single layer in a shallow non-metallic dish.

2 Mix together all the other ingredients except the oil and pour over the meat, turning to coat well. Cover with plastic wrap and refrigerate overnight, turning occasionally.

3 Drain the ribs, reserving the marinade, and cook them over medium heat on a lightly oiled barbecue grill or flat plate. Baste often with the marinade and cook for 15–20 minutes, or until the ribs are tender and well browned, turning occasionally. Season to taste and serve immediately.

INGREDIENTS

8 large fresh sardines
8 sprigs lemon thyme
3 tablespoons extra virgin olive oil
2 garlic cloves, crushed
1 teaspoon finely grated lemon zest
2 tablespoons lemon juice
1 teaspoon ground cumin
lemon wedges, for serving

1   Carefully slit the sardines from head to tail and remove the gut. Rinse, then pat dry inside
    and out with paper towels. Place a sprig of lemon thyme in each fish cavity and arrange
    the fish in a shallow non-metallic dish.

2   Combine the olive oil, garlic, lemon zest, lemon juice and cumin and pour over the fish.
    Cover and refrigerate for 2 hours.

3   Cook the sardines on a hot, lightly oiled barbecue flat plate, basting frequently with the
    marinade, for about 2–3 minutes each side or until the flesh flakes easily when tested
    with a fork. Alternatively, barbecue in a sardine cooking rack until tender. Serve hot with
    lemon wedges.

INGREDIENTS

100 g (3^1/$_2$ oz) butter, softened
2 garlic cloves, crushed
100 g (3^1/$_2$ oz) Blue Castello cheese
2 teaspoons finely shredded sage leaves
1 kg (2 lb 4 oz) beef eye fillet (thick end), trimmed
1 tablespoon olive oil

1   To make the blue cheese butter, mash together the softened butter, garlic, cheese and
    sage until they are well combined. Form the mixture into a log and wrap it in baking paper,
    twisting the ends to seal them. Refrigerate the butter until firm, then cut it into 5 mm
    (^{1}/$_4$ inch) slices and leave it at room temperature until needed.

2   Cut the beef into four thick, equal pieces and tie a piece of string around the edge of each
    so it will keep its shape during cooking. Brush both sides of each steak with the oil and
    season with freshly ground pepper. Heat a barbecue to medium–high direct heat and
    cook the beef on the chargrill plate for 6–7 minutes each side for medium, or to your
    liking.

3   Put two slices of blue cheese butter on top of each steak as soon as you remove it from
    the barbecue and remove the string.

NOTE   Any leftover butter can be wrapped in baking paper and foil, and frozen for up to 2 months.
    It is also delicious with chicken and pork.

INGREDIENTS

4 lamb chump chops, about 250 g (9 oz) each
2 tablespoons lemon juice

Citrus filling

3 spring onions (scallions), finely chopped
1 celery stalk, finely chopped
2 teaspoons grated fresh ginger
60 g (³/₄ cup) fresh breadcrumbs
2 tablespoons orange juice
2 teaspoons finely grated orange zest
1 teaspoon chopped rosemary

1 Cut a deep, long pocket in the side of each lamb chop. Mix together the spring onion, celery, ginger, breadcrumbs, orange juice, zest and rosemary and spoon into the pockets in the lamb.

2 Cook on a hot, lightly oiled barbecue flat plate or grill, turning once, for 15 minutes, or until the lamb is cooked through but still pink in the centre. Drizzle with the lemon juice before serving.

LAMB CHOPS WITH CITRUS POCKETS

LOBSTER WITH BURNT BUTTER SAUCE AND GRILLED LEMON

150 g (5^1/$_2$ oz) butter
60 ml (^{1}/$_4$ cup) lemon juice
2 tablespoons chopped flat-leaf (Italian) parsley
1 small garlic clove, crushed
8 lobster tails in the shell
2 lemons, cut into wedges

1 Melt the butter in a small saucepan over medium heat and cook it for 3 minutes or until it begins to brown, but watch it carefully to make sure that it doesn't burn. Lower the heat, and cook the butter for another 2 minutes, or until it is a dark, golden brown. Remove the pan from the heat, add the lemon juice, parsley and garlic, and season with salt and freshly ground black pepper.

2 Cut the lobster tails lengthways and remove any digestive tract, but leave the meat in the shell. Preheat a barbecue chargrill plate to medium direct heat and brush the exposed lobster meat with lots of the butter mixture. Cook the lobster tails, cut-side down, on the chargrill plate for 6 minutes, then turn them over and cook for another 3–5 minutes, or until the shells turn bright red. While the lobster is cooking, put the lemon wedges on the hottest part of the chargrill and cook them for 1 minute on each side, or until they are marked and heated through. Arrange the lobster on a serving plate and serve it with the grilled lemon wedges and the rest of the warm brown butter as a dipping sauce. This is delicious with a green salad and some crusty bread to soak up the juices.

INGREDIENTS

60 ml (^{1}/$_4$ cup) sesame oil
60 ml (^{1}/$_4$ cup) soy sauce
2 garlic cloves, crushed
2 tablespoons grated fresh ginger
1 tablespoon lemon juice
2 tablespoons chopped spring onions (scallions)
60 g (^{1}/$_3$ cup) soft brown sugar
500 g (1 lb 2 oz) beef fillet

1 Combine the sesame oil, soy sauce, garlic, ginger, lemon juice, spring onion and brown sugar in a non-metallic dish. Add the beef and coat well with the marinade. Cover and refrigerate for at least 2 hours, or overnight if possible.

2 Brown the beef on all sides on a very hot, lightly oiled barbecue grill or flat plate. When the beef is sealed, remove, wrap in foil and return to the barbecue, turning occasionally, for a further 15–20 minutes, depending on how well done you like your meat. Leave for 10 minutes before slicing.

3 Put the leftover marinade in a small saucepan and boil for 5 minutes. This is delicious served as a sauce with the beef.

SESAME AND GINGER BEEF

INGREDIENTS

$^1/_4$ cup (60 ml/2 fl oz) lime juice
2 tablespoons fish sauce
2 tablespoons sweet chilli sauce
2 teaspoons grated palm sugar
1 teaspoon sesame oil
1 clove garlic, finely chopped
1 tablespoon virgin olive oil
4 tuna steaks (150 g/5 oz each), at room temperature
200 g (7 oz) dried thin wheat noodles
6 spring onions, thinly sliced
$^3/_4$ cup (25 g/1 oz) chopped fresh coriander leaves
lime wedges, to garnish

1   To make the dressing, place the lime juice, fish sauce, chilli sauce, sugar, sesame oil and garlic in a small bowl and mix together.

2   Heat the olive oil in a chargrill pan. Add the tuna steaks and cook over high heat for 2 minutes each side, or until cooked to your liking. Transfer the steaks to a warm plate, cover and keep warm.

3   Place the noodles in a large saucepan of lightly salted, rapidly boiling water and return to the boil. Cook for 4 minutes, or until the noodles are tender. Drain well. Add half the dressing and half the spring onion and coriander to the noodles and gently toss together.

4   Either cut the tuna into even cubes or slice it.

5   Place the noodles on serving plates and top with the tuna. Mix the remaining dressing with the spring onion and coriander and drizzle over the tuna. Garnish with lime wedges.

NOTE   If you prefer, you can serve the tuna steaks whole rather than cutting them into cubes. If serving whole, they would look better served with the noodles on the side.

1 kg raw medium prawns (shrimp)

3 teaspoons hot paprika

2 teaspoons ground cumin

1 cup (30 g/1 oz) firmly packed fresh flat-leaf parsley

$^1/_2$ cup (15 g/$^1/_2$ oz) firmly packed fresh coriander (cilantro) leaves

100 ml ($3^1/_2$ fl oz) lemon juice

145 ml (5 fl oz) olive oil

$1^1/_2$ cups (280 g/10 oz) couscous

1 tablespoon grated lemon rind

lemon wedges, to serve

1   Peel the prawns, leaving the tails intact. Gently pull out the dark vein from the backs, starting at the head end. Place the prawns in a large bowl. Dry-fry the paprika and cumin in a frying pan for about 1 minute, or until fragrant. Remove from the heat.

2   Blend or process the spices, parsley, coriander, lemon juice and $^1/_2$ cup (125 ml/$4^1/_4$ fl oz) of the oil until finely chopped. Add a little salt and pepper. Pour over the prawns and mix well, then cover with plastic wrap and refrigerate for 10 minutes. Heat a chargrill pan or barbecue plate to hot.

3   Meanwhile, to cook the couscous, bring 1 cup (250 ml/8 fl oz) water to the boil in a saucepan, then stir in the couscous, lemon rind, the remaining oil and $^1/_4$ teaspoon salt. Remove from the heat, cover and leave for 5 minutes. Fluff the couscous with a fork, adding a little extra olive oil if needed.

4   Cook the prawns on the chargrill pan for about 3–4 minutes, or until cooked through, turning and brushing with extra marinade while cooking (take care not to overcook). Serve the prawns on a bed of couscous, with a wedge of lemon.

BARBECUED CHERMOULA PRAWNS

4 tablespoons fresh mint leaves
1 tablespoon fresh flat-leaf parsley
2 cloves garlic
$1^1/_2$ tablespoons lemon rind (white pith removed), cut into thin strips
2 tablespoons extra virgin olive oil
8 French-trimmed lamb cutlets
2 carrots
2 zucchini (courgettes)
1 tablespoon lemon juice

1 To make the gremolata, finely chop the mint, parsley, garlic and lemon strips, then combine well.

2 Heat a chargrill pan or barbecue plate to very hot. Lightly brush with 1 tablespoon of the oil. Cook the cutlets over medium heat for 2 minutes on each side, or until cooked to your liking. Remove the cutlets and cover to keep warm.

3 Trim the ends from the carrots and zucchini and, using a sharp vegetable peeler, peel the vegetables lengthways into ribbons. Heat the remaining oil in a large saucepan, add the vegetables and toss over medium heat for 3–5 minutes, or until sautéed but tender.

4 Divide the cutlets among the serving plates, sprinkle the cutlets with the gremolata and drizzle with the lemon juice. Serve with the vegetable ribbons.

350 g (12¹/₄ oz) angel hair pasta

100 g (3¹/₂ oz) butter

3 cloves garlic, crushed

24 scallops, without roe

150 g (5¹/₄ oz) baby rocket leaves

2 teaspoons finely grated lemon rind

¹/₄ cup (60 ml/2 fl oz) lemon juice

125 g (4¹/₂ oz) semi-dried (sun-blushed) tomatoes, thinly sliced

30 g shaved Parmesan

1 Cook the pasta in a large saucepan of boiling water until *al dente*. Meanwhile, melt the butter in a small saucepan, add the garlic and cook over low heat, stirring, for 1 minute. Remove from the heat.

2 Heat a lightly greased chargrill plate over high heat and cook the scallops, brushing occasionally with some of the garlic butter for 1–2 minutes each side, or until cooked. Set aside and keep warm.

3 Drain the pasta and return to the pan with the remaining garlic butter, the rocket, lemon rind, lemon juice and tomato and toss until combined. Divide among four serving plates and top with the scallops. Season to taste and sprinkle with Parmesan.

ANGEL HAIR PASTA WITH SCALLOPS AND ROCKET

CAJUN CHICKEN WITH FRESH TOMATO AND CORN SALSA

2 corn cobs

2 vine-ripened tomatoes, diced

1 Lebanese cucumber, diced

2 tablespoons roughly chopped fresh coriander (cilantro) leaves

4 chicken breast fillets (about 200 g/7 oz each)

$1/4$ cup (35 g/1$1/4$ oz) Cajun seasoning

2 tablespoons lime juice

lime wedges, to serve

1 Cook the corn cobs in a saucepan of boiling water for 5 minutes, or until tender. Remove the kernels using a sharp knife and place in a bowl with the tomato, cucumber and coriander. Season and mix well.

2 Heat a chargrill pan or barbecue plate to medium heat and brush lightly with oil. Pound each chicken breast between two sheets of plastic wrap with a mallet or rolling pin until 2 cm ($3/4$ inch) thick. Lightly coat the chicken with the Cajun seasoning and shake off any excess. Cook for 5 minutes on each side, or until just cooked through.

3 Just before serving, stir the lime juice into the salsa. Place a chicken breast on each plate and spoon the salsa on the side. Serve with the lime wedges, a green salad and crusty bread.

INGREDIENTS

3 teaspoons finely grated fresh ginger

$^1/_2$ cup (25 g/1 oz) chopped fresh coriander (cilantro) leaves

$1^1/_2$ teaspoons grated lime rind

$^1/_3$ cup (80 ml/2$^3/_4$ fl oz) lime juice

4 skinless chicken breast fillets (about 750 g/26$^1/_2$ oz), trimmed

$1^1/_4$ cups (250 g/9 oz) jasmine rice

2 tablespoons oil

3 zucchini (courgettes), cut into wedges

4 large flat mushrooms, stalks trimmed

1   Combine the ginger, coriander, lime rind and 2 tablespoons of the lime juice. Spread 2 teaspoons of the herb mixture over each fillet and season well. Marinate for 1 hour. Combine the remaining herb mixture with the remaining lime juice in a screwtop jar. Set aside until needed.

2   Bring a large saucepan of water to the boil. Add the rice and cook for 12 minutes, stirring occasionally. Drain well.

3   Meanwhile, heat a chargrill pan or barbecue plate to medium—this will take about 5 minutes and lightly brush with oil. Brush the zucchini and mushrooms with the remaining oil. Place the chicken on the chargrill and cook on each side for 4–5 minutes, or until cooked through. Add the vegetables during the last 5 minutes of cooking, and turn frequently until browned on the outside and just softened. Cover with foil until ready to serve.

4   Divide the rice among four serving bowls. Cut the chicken fillets into long thick strips, then arrange on top of the rice. Shake the dressing well and drizzle over the chicken and serve with the chargrilled vegetables.

PORK WITH APPLE AND ONION WEDGES

2 pork fillets, about 400 g (14 oz) each

12 pitted prunes

2 green apples, cored, unpeeled, cut into wedges

2 red onions, cut into wedges

50 g (1³/₄ oz) butter, melted

2 teaspoons caster (superfine) sugar

125 ml (¹/₂ cup) cream

2 tablespoons brandy

1 tablespoon chopped chives

1 Trim the pork of any excess fat and sinew and cut each fillet in half. Make a slit with a knife through the centre of each fillet and push 3 prunes into each one. Brush the pork, the apple and onion wedges with the melted butter and sprinkle the apple and onion with the caster sugar.

2 Brown the pork on a hot, lightly oiled barbecue flat plate. Add the apple and onion wedges (you may need to cook in batches if your flat plate isn't large enough). Cook, turning frequently, for 5–7 minutes, or until the pork is cooked through and the apple and onion pieces are softened. Remove the pork, apple and onion from the barbecue and keep warm.

3 Mix together the cream, brandy and chives in a pan. Transfer to the stove top and simmer for 3 minutes, or until slightly thickened. Season with salt and black pepper.

4 Slice the meat and serve with the apple, onion wedges and brandy cream sauce.

All our recipes are thoroughly tested in a specially developed test kitchen. Standard metric measuring cups and spoons are used in the development of our recipes. All cup and spoon measurements are level. We have used 60 g (2¼ oz/Grade 3) eggs in all recipes. Sizes of cans vary from manufacturer to manufacturer and between countries – use the can size closest to the one suggested in the recipe.

CONVERSION GUIDE

1 cup = 250 ml (9 fl oz)

1 teaspoon = 5 ml

1 Australian tablespoon = 20 ml (4 teaspoons)

1 UK/US tablespoon = 15 ml (3 teaspoons)

DRY MEASURES

30 g = 1 oz

250 g = 9 oz

500 g = 1 lb 2 oz

LIQUID MEASURES

30 ml = 1 fl oz

125 ml = 4 fl oz

250 ml = 9 fl oz

LINEAR MEASURES

6 mm = ¼ inch

1 cm = ½ inch

2.5 cm = 1 inch

CUP CONVERSIONS – DRY INGREDIENTS

1 cup almonds, slivered whole = 125 g (4½ oz)

1 cup cheese, lightly packed processed cheddar = 155 g (5½ oz)

1 cup wheat flour = 125 g (4½ oz)

1 cup wholemeal flour = 140 g (5 oz)

1 cup minced (ground) meat = 250 g (9 oz)

1 cup pasta shapes = 125 g (4½ oz)

1 cup raisins = 170 g (6 oz)

1 cup rice, short grain, raw = 200 g (7 oz)

1 cup sesame seeds = 160 g (6 oz)

1 cup split peas = 250 g (9 oz)

INTERNATIONAL GLOSSARY

capsicum	sweet bell pepper
chick pea	garbanzo bean
chilli	chile, chili pepper
cornflour	cornstarch
eggplant	aubergine
spring onion	scallion
zucchini	courgette
plain flour	all-purpose flour
prawns	shrimp
minced meat	ground meat

Where temperature ranges are indicated, the lower figure applies to gas ovens, the higher to electric ovens. This allows for the fact that the flame in gas ovens generates a drier heat, which effectively cooks food faster than the moister heat of an electric oven, even if the temperature setting is the same.

	°C	°F	GAS MARK
Very slow	120	250	½
Slow	150	300	2
Mod slow	160	325	3
Moderate	180	350	4
Mod hot	190(g)–210(e)	375–425	5
Hot	200(g)–240(e)	400–475	6
Very hot	230(g)–260(e)	450–525	8

INDEX

191

Published in 2006 by Bay Books,
an imprint of Murdoch Books Pty Limited.

ISBN 1-74045-938-5
978-1-74045-938-9

Printed by Sing Cheong Printing Company Ltd.
Printed in China.